# Let's Play!

## Promoting Active Playgrounds

**Jane Watkinson, PhD**

**University of Manitoba**

**University of Alberta (Professor Emeritus)**

**Human Kinetics**

**Library of Congress Cataloging-in-Publication Data**

Watkinson, Jane, 1948-
   Let's play! : promoting active playgrounds / Jane Watkinson.
      p. cm.
   Includes bibliographical references and index.
   ISBN-13: 978-0-7360-7001-0 (soft cover)
   ISBN-10: 0-7360-7001-X (soft cover)
   1. Playgrounds. 2. Playgrounds--Social aspects. 3. Play--Social aspects. 4. Child development.
5. Social interaction in children. 6. Social skills in children. I. Title.
   GV423.W38 2010
   796.06'8--dc22

                              2009018664

ISBN-10: 0-7360-7001-X
ISBN-13: 978-0-7360-7001-0

The Web addresses cited in this text were current as of June 2009, unless otherwise noted.

**Acquisitions Editor:** Gayle Kassing, PhD; **Developmental Editor:** Jacqueline Eaton Blakley; **Assistant Editor:** Anne Rumery; **Copyeditor:** Tom Tiller; **Indexer:** Alisha Jeddeloh; **Graphic Designer:** Fred Starbird; **Graphic Artist:** Denise Lowry; **Cover Designer:** Keith Blomberg; **Art Manager:** Kelly Hendren; **Associate Art Manager:** Alan L. Wilborn; **Illustrator (cover and interior):** Terry Watkinson; **Printer:** Versa Press

Printed in the United States of America        10  9  8  7  6  5  4  3  2  1

The paper in this book is certified under a sustainable forestry program.

**Human Kinetics**
Web site: www.HumanKinetics.com

*United States:* Human Kinetics, P.O. Box 5076, Champaign, IL 61825-5076
800-747-4457
e-mail: humank@hkusa.com

*Canada:* Human Kinetics, 475 Devonshire Road Unit 100, Windsor, ON N8Y 2L5
800-465-7301 (in Canada only)
e-mail: info@hkcanada.com

*Europe:* Human Kinetics, 107 Bradford Road, Stanningley, Leeds LS28 6AT, United Kingdom
+44 (0) 113 255 5665
e-mail: hk@hkeurope.com

*Australia:* Human Kinetics, 57A Price Avenue, Lower Mitcham, South Australia 5062
08 8372 0999
e-mail: info@hkaustralia.com

*New Zealand:* Human Kinetics, Division of Sports Distributors NZ Ltd., P.O. Box 300 226 Albany, North Shore City, Auckland
0064 9 448 1207
e-mail: info@humankinetics.co.nz

E4175

# Contents

# Preface

**W**hat do children love to do the most? Play! They especially love being on the playground before and after school and at recess time. It's their favorite time of day, but it's also a critical opportunity to engage in physical and social activity.

So it is disturbing for many reasons that some children do not, or cannot, take part in common playground activities. Withdrawal or exclusion from play can lead to social isolation, unhealthy choices, and low self-esteem. We know that children spend less and less time in physical activity at home, where the TV and the computer may be more attractive leisure options. This means they may go to school without the skills or practice they need in order to be active participants. But social and physical participation on the playground is important for them—to ensure healthy habits, to reduce the likelihood of childhood obesity, and to increase the likelihood that they will make friends and become part of the active social groups that form in unstructured free time.

Being physically active starts early in life, and having the skills required for physical activity is critical. This book and CD-ROM, based on the Let's Play! program, prepare you to ensure that every child you know has a repertoire of movement skills to be active on the playground. The book includes a checklist of important activities that children play between the ages of 3 and 8, a friendly method of assessing the specific skills required for taking part in these activities, and simple tips for teaching playground skills and games.

The Let's Play! program was developed in the Pat Austin Research Lab at the University of Alberta over many years. The research program investigated the movement skills and play patterns of children ages 3 to 8, as well as their perceptions about their own competence and their motivations for engaging in play on the playground. During the course of our research, we discovered answers to many of the questions that concern parents, teachers, day-care professionals, and recreation leaders on a daily basis.

And we have a lot of good news to share! First, every kid *wants* to be active. Second, every kid *can* be active, regardless of ability level. And finally, we have created a friendly, intuitive method for identifying how to help kids who are not fully engaged in play with their peers to improve their skills!

The methods presented in this book rely on the common sense of teachers and parents; expertise in physical activity or sport is not a requirement. And these methods are actually fun! They feature a device for screening children to determine if they are doing what their peers do on the playground (the *playmap*) and assessment checklists organized by equipment (called the *playlists*) that will help parents and teachers look closely at individual children to see what they can and can't do on the playground.

The initial screening requires that children simply play for a period of time, then report their activities using illustrated materials that are easy for them to understand. Children whose screening shows that they are not fully participating in play with their peers can be further assessed in naturalistic settings, with other children present, and preferably in the midst of free play. Follow-up interventions employ a simple teacher-helping system that has been used with children with and without disabilities during the course of the Let's Play! research (Watkinson & Wall, 1982a). The assessment protocol itself is consistent with individualized instructional techniques and can guide the instruction of movement skills by teachers who lack specific training in movement skills.

This is the first book in the physical activity field to provide an assessment protocol for children's gross motor play on the playground. The playground is the most universal play space for children in the United States and Canada, yet participation at recess has been taken for granted until now. We assume that every child can play, but children need movement skills to take part in unstructured free play on playground equipment. This book has unique features that will help you make a difference in the play time of the children you know:

- Attractive and original illustrations appeal to parents, teachers, and children.

- A protocol allows for the screening of 30 children in 30 minutes to help you identify children who are not actively participating during free time on the playground. This protocol uses children's own reports of their activity, an after-recess activity that is fun.

- An assessment protocol details the specific skills needed for the activities. It allows testing to be carried out in the midst of regular outdoor play without disruption.

- Materials are designed for teachers and parents who have no specific training. These are based on illustrations rather than written material, so there is little time needed for preparation.

- A specialized method identifies children who are at risk of isolation in play and a method of intervening (without labeling) helps them acquire skills.

- A large inventory of exciting skills and activities—developed with children and tested with children—stimulates playground activity.

Adults who work with young children devote plenty of time to teaching them letters and numbers. Although this is important, from a social perspective the most important period of the day for children is on the playground, where friendships are made and children become part of social groups. Children need to learn a range of movement skills that allow them to take part. Classroom teachers, child-care workers, physical educators, adapted physical educators, physiotherapists, occupational therapists, recreational leaders, and parents will find this book useful because they will recognize the importance of arming their children with play skills and they will find the illustrations attractive and easy to understand.

The book will also be of interest to physical educators, playground supervisors, recreation therapists, physiotherapists, and occupational therapists concerned with the development of movement skills in children who have special needs or are at risk of social isolation.

Concerned parents of children ages 3 to 8 will also be interested in this book since it is easy to apply in children's daily lives. Playground skill assessments are informal and can be carried out unobtrusively by parents at local playgrounds. Furthermore, the assessments do not lead to labeling or direct comparison to other children but rather to the identification of skills that can be learned or practiced so that children can use them every day on the playground. For parents of average, gifted, or athletic children, there is a wide range of activities to encourage. These children can see pictures of other youngsters doing skills that they might like to try next time they go to the playground. Parents of children with disabilities will find illustrations of a wide range of skills that children can learn that will allow them to move confidently on the playground.

For children, play really matters. The playground is their world. With the *Let's Play!* book and CD-ROM, the adults who care about them are equipped to make that world a better place, one child at a time.

# How to Use This Book and CD-ROM

The Let's Play! program is for caring adults who want to help children acquire the skills they need to take part in everyday playground activity, whether it is at recess, at day care, or at the neighborhood park. This book explains how to identify the children who need help, determine what kind of help they need, and methodically work with them to strengthen areas of weakness that prevent participation.

The accompanying CD-ROM includes assessment forms that are integral to the program and discussed in the book. These forms are the means of identifying who needs help and what kind of help is needed. Follow the instructions found in the back of the book to best access the files. Once you have them open, you can print them on 8.5 x 11 paper to use as you wish.

You will find the following forms on the CD-ROM:

- Preschool playmap (to use with children approximately 3 to 5 years old)

- Grade-school playmap (to use with children approximately 6 to 8 years old)

- Playlists organized by equipment or skill (slide, bars, or swing, for example)

- Blank playlist (which may be customized by pasting in illustrations included on the CD-ROM)

- Blank report card (which may be customized by pasting in illustrations included on the CD-ROM)

You can print as many copies of the forms as you need, depending on your situation. For example, if you are trying to determine which playground equipment your four-year-old daughter is able to use and prefers, you can print one preschool playmap to take with you to the playground as you observe. Or say you are a first-grade teacher interested in knowing which of your 25 students are not actively engaged on the playground; you can print 25 copies of the grade-school playmap so that each student can indicate after a play period which activities he or she chose, then you can print another playmap to tabulate the students' responses and discover which activities are most important for this class—and who is being left out.

In addition, some of the forms can be customized to your needs. For example, you can create a playlist that shows the specific skills you want to work on with a child by opening the blank playlist form, copying illustrations that show the desired skills, and pasting them into the blank form and saving it. Teachers or children's program leaders can also copy and paste illustrations from the playlists and playmaps into the sample report card form in order to create individualized report cards to share with their students' parents.

The book and CD-ROM have been designed to work together to guide you through the process of helping kids become full participants in the vital context of the local playground. By helping them develop the skills to participate, you are helping them develop the social tools needed for a happy childhood and the physical tools needed for an active lifestyle that lasts well into adulthood.

# Acknowledgments

I wish to acknowledge first, the many children, parents, and teachers from Edmonton, Alberta, Wolfville, Nova Scotia, and Winnipeg, Manitoba, who played with us on their playgrounds and were participants in our research program over the years.

Students who have contributed to this research program include Sharon Baker, Karen Calzonetti, Janice Causgrove Dunn, Jamie Covey, Sean Dwyer, David Fitzpatrick, Donna Goodwin, Sarah Hilton, Christina Lau, Andreea Mohora, Sue Muloin, Nancy Spencer-Cavaliere, Denise Wagner, and Larry Wilhelm. Their ideas, energy, and commitment to the happiness of children at play kept the research program moving forward over many years.

Former colleagues made substantial contributions both through their ideas and their advice to students as the research program unfolded: Marcel Bouffard, Janice Causgrove Dunn, Brian Nielsen, and Linda Thompson.

I want to acknowledge most particularly the insights and experiences of my son, Andrew Terry Watkinson, whose stories of life on the playground were daily tests of the theoretical underpinnings of the research program.

The research leading to this book has been generously supported by the Social Sciences and Humanities Research Council of Canada and the University of Alberta Small Faculties Research Fund.

# CHAPTER 1

# Understanding the Value of Play

There is little debate about the importance of free play for children. The very fact that dozens of new playgrounds are built every year in our communities indicates that we believe they are valuable additions to our schools and neighborhoods. Parents take their children to the playground regularly. Day-care providers build outdoor play time into every morning and afternoon and sometimes lead little caravans of children (hooked together for safety) along blocks of sidewalk to get to a good playground. Schools also provide regular recess times on the playground at least two times a day, with another free-play time at lunch. Thus we clearly hold a firm belief in the importance of free play in a child's day—especially the kind of whole-body activity that occurs on outdoor playgrounds. And for most children, playground time is the best time of the day!

It is common to hear statements about the importance of free-play time. Books abound that advocate free time as being critical to a child's development in all areas of life: social, emotional, physical, and cognitive. Some suggest that freedom to play may help children learn to interact better with their peers, learn rules, learn self-discipline, and learn to understand their fellow human beings. Others argue that games with lots of rules offer children an opportunity to acquire "social intelligence" by prompting them to practice using skills such as supervising (when leading a game), negotiating (when making up rules for an informal game), organizing (when deciding who should play which position on a team), and persuading (when handling disagreements about whether someone has broken the rules). Such skills may serve a child well later in life. Others say that during play children learn to express themselves, establish and maintain friendships, solve problems, accept responsibility, and persevere. Playing outside is also believed by many to help children pay attention when they go back into the classroom.

"We have talked to many children about their lives on the playground. What they say can help us understand their perspectives, values, feelings, and thoughts about their play engagement. The quotes in this book come from children who are 6 to 8 years of age, in grades 1 to 3, who may or may not be having difficulty on the playground. We often asked these children questions about "another child just like you" so the children being interviewed didn't have to reveal too much about themselves directly. We did this to make it easier for them to talk about things."

While such claims may sometimes be a bit exaggerated, a compelling case can be made for the importance of free play in children's lives. We know from studies of orphanages in developing countries, for example, that children can experience developmental difficulties if they fail to have opportunities to play. So we might support free play because we think it is a sacred right of children. We might also use it as a reward for good behavior. We might be convinced that free play helps our children engage constructively in class. We might understand that active play helps children develop skills of diplomacy. And of course free play can be challenging for the body as well. Playing on the playground can help children develop movement skills and give them opportunities to use those skills. In all of this, it is crucial to recognize that play skills are necessary in order for children to play vigorously enough to experience health benefits and gain entry into the games and social activities of other children.

# PHYSICAL BENEFITS

Playgrounds are built to encourage many kinds of movement that push kids to make their bodies work hard at having fun. Slides and climbers just beg children to climb up and slide down, bars and horizontal ladders invite hanging, and open space between the equipment calls for running and jumping. We wouldn't necessarily refer to such structures as "exercise equipment," but that is precisely what they are—equipment that invites exercise of all kinds for young people. Unlike the treadmills and elliptical steppers that we adults often buy for our own exercise, playground equipment accommodates many forms of movement and is able to withstand the activities that children dream up as they grow older and try new things. The slide is not just for going down; you can also pull yourself *up* the slide. You can climb up the edges of the spiral slide. You can sit on top of the tube slide. These various activities require children to use different muscles and muscle groups, thus producing the exercise that is necessary for the development of strong bodies. Muscles improve with use; the more they are pushed, the stronger they get.

Children don't even notice the stresses and strains that are being put on their muscles, their lungs, and their hearts as they move around the playground. But this is serious business for children's health. Experts recommend that children get 60 minutes of moderate or vigorous physical activity each day. *Moderate* activity involves breathing more heavily than usual but not to the point of feeling tired. You can usually keep talking when you do moderate activity, such as walking, bouncing a ball, hanging or swinging on a bar, or throwing and catching. When doing moderate activity, you may not notice that your heart rate is increased, but it is—and this is good for you. *Vigorous* activity involves a fast breathing rate and a high heart rate; it's the kind of activity where you can feel your heart thumping or where you can't talk because you are out of breath. Running, jumping, or climbing a ladder quickly can make us feel this way. We need daily bouts of moderate *and* vigorous activity in order to become and stay healthy. We can achieve this goal through one long bout of activity or through shorter but more frequent periods of activity such as those provided by recess breaks.

The playground, then, is a good place for children to look after their health. It is where the majority of active play takes place. It can be hard for children to be really active at home unless they have a big backyard or a quiet street to run on, but a playground invites children to run and jump and play, and children typically are more active there. In fact, children are even more likely to be vigorously active on a playground than in physical education or exercise classes. At least this seems to be true for boys. If you watch children as they enter the playground, you see a great burst of high-energy activity during the first few minutes before they settle into less vigorous forms of play. During recess, children are generally active for about 30 percent to 60 percent of their time on the playground. The percentage increases if they have to wait a long time until recess or if they are bored in class before recess begins.

Free-play time is often in jeopardy as adults strive to fill children's days with more reading, writing, and arithmetic. The American Academy of Pediatrics says that half of elementary-age children do not get enough daily physical activity to benefit their hearts and lungs. We should be increasing—not decreasing—the amount of free-play time our kids have. One way to do so is to provide frequent recess periods at school, but this alone does not provide the recommended daily amount of moderate and vigorous physical activity for children. In fact, since children are usually active for only part of a given recess period, such periods provide only about 20 percent of the needed vigorous activity.

In light of the health benefits of free play on the playground, it is clearly not a good strategy for parents or teachers to offer recess or play time as a reward or to reduce it as a punishment. Play time is critical to health. It is extremely important to the growth and development of the heart, lungs, muscles, and bones of the body. Therefore, it should be protected. We would not withdraw opportunities to practice reading or writing or arithmetic as a punishment for poor behavior. Free play needs to be treated with the same respect. It is just as important, if not more so, because it is critical to good health.

Many people are concerned about obesity rates in North America, and parents may worry about a child's weight or size. Obesity does not result entirely from lack of physical activity; other factors, such as nutrition, play a very important role. But daily physical activity—including both vigorous and moderate periods of play—can contribute to a healthy body size, and children who are overweight can still have a healthy heart if they are active regularly. We should work to ensure that they get the recommended 60 minutes. To take advantage of such opportunities, though, children need a good repertoire of movement skills. Recent evidence says that children who are not skilled will not be as fit and healthy as children who are highly skilled.

Parents might be tempted to make children exercise by doing regular workouts like many adults do. Our advice would be quite different: Give an overweight child many opportunities to be active on a playground. The same goal will be met, but with a better chance that the child will sustain the activity because it is enjoyable. The American Academy of Pediatrics (AAP) believes that adult structuring of free play denies children the opportunity to be independent and resourceful. The AAP also says that adult intervention can interfere with children's improvement of physical fitness because children are not as active when supervised. Many professional groups, such as the National Association of Early Childhood Specialists in State Departments of Education and the National Association for Sport and Physical Education, recommend *free* play on the playground every day, in addition to teacher-directed physical education in school.

# SOCIAL BENEFITS

Playing alone can be enjoyable, and most children spend some time alone at play, even when other children are nearby. This is not something for parents or teachers to worry about. However, as children mature, they do play together more and more, and being good at movement skills is important for playing with others, especially as children get older. In the classroom, things are different. Being good at math, reading, or writing may not enhance a child's social acceptance or ability to build friendships. In fact, during the later school years, exceptional talent in classroom activities may even lead to lower degrees of acceptance and status for some children. Overall, doing well academically in school is usually unrelated to having friends. But doing well in playground games and activities is important to having friends, especially for boys. Competence in doing activities such as running, playing tag, throwing a ball, and playing soccer is strongly and positively related to social acceptance. Skilled children are often the most valued friends on the playground, and children without movement competence are less likely to be socially accepted. This seems to be the very hard fact of life on the playground.

"**Chloe, age 8: If you're playing a team game, like soccer, where you have to run, then if somebody wants to play who's really bad at soccer, they might argue about who gets what player because they think . . . if one person is bad on the team, because they don't know what to do, then everybody else basically won't have any [fun]. . . . [I]t's like a puzzle with one piece missing, because the whole team has to be good and work together . . . and if somebody doesn't have those skills then . . . they might not be wanted to play on some of these teams.**"

It is not just the doing of a skill that is important but also the speed and efficiency with which it is done. One child may be able to climb the steps to the top of the slide, but another child who can do it *quickly* and *smoothly* in order to avoid being tagged is granted a special status by peers. It is a sad truth that children who lack movement competence tend to be less popular and have fewer friends. In fact, children who lack playground competence can become isolated at school, and this isolation is damaging to their self-esteem.

Skilled children, on the other hand, become informal playground leaders and thus gain experience in decision making and choice making that may not be available to children who are less skilled. For example, athletic boys in elementary school typically assume dominant roles in activities on the playground at recess. They often control who can and cannot participate in games, whereas children who are left out of an activity have no say in who does, or does not, take part. Exclusion leads to even less practice of the skills required for inclusion, thus exacerbating the situation. This is why children with poor movement competence need to be identified early in their lives and helped to develop sufficient skill to gain entry into play activity before the cycle of exclusion, loneliness, and lack of practice takes hold.

Being left out is very hard to handle. When children don't play, when they withdraw or are excluded, they can experience long-lasting negative effects on their feelings about themselves. Their memories of their time on the playground will be vivid and painful. Children who withdraw will lose the opportunity to practice the skills needed to be active on the playground, and this loss can start a cycle of inactivity that may last for years. In fact, experts think this cycle may be one cause of obesity, and it certainly lies at the heart of children's isolation from peers.

We often make assumptions that all children can automatically play on the playground, but a significant number of children are isolated and inactive. Some of these children feel they are not skilled enough to take part. Others are worried about being hurt by flying balls or falling from climbers. Children with mild to severe disability are often intentionally left out of playground activity, and this exclusion is hurtful and damaging to their feelings of self-worth. Some children are deliberately excluded because their movement and social skills don't measure up to the expectations of their peers. Whatever the reason for being uninvolved, this lack of participation can lead to a cycle of developmental problems: lack of practice, increasing deficits in movement and social skills, lack of fitness, unhealthy bodies, and few friends. Most important, being left out can lead to sadness and loneliness.

# WHAT CAN ADULTS DO TO HELP?

To engage in play, children must have sufficient movement competence to be accepted into their peer group activities. The key is sufficient skill. We need to ensure that children have sufficient skill before they enter school. We also need to be able to identify children who lack the skills to participate during their school years and provide them with the extra teaching and practice they need in order to develop a good repertoire of skills for play. For some children, being able to do one or two things well might be enough to provide them with entry to playground activities. For most kids, though, having many skills, and being able to do them all well, is the ticket to complete engagement with their peers. So they need a *repertoire* of skills that they can do, and the broader and deeper this repertoire is the more movement success they will have on the playground.

A good skill repertoire does not, however, appear automatically: The more free-play time available to children, the greater the chance that their repertoire will expand. It takes practice and opportunity; for some children, it also takes instruction and coaching.

## *The Right Repertoire for a Child's Age*

Very young children may start to acquire playground skills by learning how to go down a wide slide into the arms of their parents. They may walk across a suspended bridge while holding a big brother's hand. They may climb a small ladder with wide rungs. A very young child may simply find it fun to hide under the climber, to run from one piece of equipment to another, or to be put into a baby swing. These activities all serve as first steps in playground skill development—and the more such activities a child can do, the better start he or she will have for life on the playground.

Even very little ones start to play alongside other children once they know how to climb the ladder and go down the slide by themselves, or hang on a bar, or pull themselves up a cargo net. Such skills allow them to play side by side with other children, to follow and lead, to take turns, to respond to other children's overtures, and to have fun all the while. Children need to be able to do some of these very basic motor skills well in order to take full advantage of playground activity.

Fortunately, many of the skills that children learn between the ages of three and seven are so exciting and fun that most children want to do them again and again. Going down a slide is exciting and often makes children want to go down repeatedly, as long as they feel reasonably safe. Later, the sensations that children feel when hanging upside down make them want to repeat the experience. When they swish through the air on a swing or zip line, they feel a kinetic sensation that is thrilling—even more so if they do it upside down! A small jump to a parent's hands as a preschooler can lead to jumping from a climbing structure. For the more daring, going airborne upon letting go of a moving swing produces a similar feeling. Many children seem to be driven to seek such thrilling experiences and to repeat them. They spin, twirl, hang, and jump, all the while getting practice at the very skills they need in order to take part in the vigorous play of the playground.

Certain skills are well learned by most children during preschool: running, jumping down from low heights, climbing ladders and stairs, going down slides, and hanging from a horizontal bar. Four- and five-year-olds chase each other, ride small vehicles, and do gymnastics maneuvers such as somersaults and taking their weight on their hands. Some can hang upside down or jump down from the stairs. Once children are in kindergarten, they learn other skills out on the playground: faster running; dodging; jumping down from greater heights; leaping over things; climbing higher ladders, as well as cargo nets and poles; and hanging from bars, ropes, and swings. Hanging from a horizontal bar develops into hanging from the knees or moving along the bar hand over hand.

During the early school years, most children build up a repertoire of such skills that they can use in many different solitary and group activities. In other words, they gain the skills to take part as they choose. They may not be Olympic performers, but they can do things well enough to participate in activities that demand certain skills. They can hang upside down without falling, run fast enough to play in a soccer game, or climb a ladder efficiently enough to keep their place in a line of children climbing to the top of the slide. They don't hold others up! If their friends run over to the spiral pole, they go there too and are able to use the pole the way the other children do (e.g., climb up it, slide down it, drop to the platform below).

Having skills that are typical of one's peers—having a broad skill repertoire to draw on when playing with them—may be the most important thing a child learns during preschool and the early school grades. Other skills, such as reading, are also fun and important, of course, but physical skills let children be part of the action.

## *Skill Repertoires for Boys and Girls*

Playground activity is important for both boys and girls. Some differences generally exist in what and where girls and boys play, and in how hard they play. But having playground skill is equally important for both.

Boys tend to be more physically active than girls are on the playground, both during and outside of school hours. For girls, recess is their most significant opportunity to be really physically active during the day. This makes recess even more important for girls than it is for boys. Thus, as a parent or teacher, you should not encourage girls to stay inside during recess or assign them caretaking activities during free-play time. Such roles may look to them like rewards for good behavior, but they actually serve as punishment for girls' bodies.

> **"K**arla, age 8, when asked about whether there are differences between boys and girls: Yep. Girls do stuff, only calm. Boys are just—running around. "

Boys' playgroups tend to be somewhat larger than girls', and girls tend to play more cooperatively; often, two or three girls spend time together, and often in less physically active ways than boys tend to play. Boys' activities are more often undertaken in larger groups in which participants compete in some sort of game. Many of these games involve vigorous running and dodging, as well as ball skills, so it is very important that boys are competent at such activities. This does not mean that it isn't important for girls to be competent at such skills as well. Girls should be encouraged to play ball games too, but they typically spend more of their time on playground equipment, and they need swinging, sliding, and monkey bar skills in order to be active participants there.

When boys and girls play together, they tend to play chasing games, such as tag, that are very good for their health. Children get a great deal of exercise during playground games that involve racing, scrambling, dodging, and sprinting; however, skipping and dancing can be just as good for the heart and lungs.

# THE UNIQUENESS OF EACH CHILD AND EACH SITUATION

Activities and games differ from school to school and from playground to playground. At one school, for example, the favorite spring game may be baseball, while at another it is hide-and-seek. Girls may play ball games against the wall at one school, whereas there may be no open wall for such an activity at another. In some areas, children need skills for snow and ice activities, but in others, of course, this is not necessary. As a result, children need a big enough skill repertoire to take up new activities in new contexts, and it is essential that they can do the things that are most typical in their own neighborhood.

When we say that boys are more active than girls or that boys play ball games more often than girls do, we mean that this is true *on average*. It does not mean that all boys are more active than all girls. The same is true when we say that free play promotes independence and getting along with others.

This may be *generally* true, but it does not mean that *all* children are necessarily learning to be independent and socially skilled. Most statements about children's play describe what groups of children do on average but not necessarily what individual children might do.

It is important for you as a parent or teacher to recognize that when claims are based on averages or group tendencies, they do not necessarily apply to all children in a group. The main goal for you is to understand how each child plays. Every child's experiences are unique, and not every instance in which a child differs from the average is a cause for concern; there is a spread around the average that is considered normal or typical. However, a child who differs *a lot* from his or her peers should be considered carefully. Addressing the needs of such a child should be of the utmost concern. It is important not to assume that children who are clumsy or who have mild, moderate, or severe disabilities are any different from their peers when it comes to wanting to play on playgrounds. They too want to be good at things so they can take part. Clarisse, who is about 9 years old and has a significant disability, becomes animated when she sees the little drawings of children doing so many things "I would like to do what that girl's doing [points to illustration of girl flipping over a bar]....at home I have a swingset and I like to swing and at first when I got it, I would ask my dad to push me and then once I got better I started [to do it myself]... And I have tried to climb up [the slide]...and I have a playhouse and a sandbox . . . usually I play all by myself. And I want to learn how to go on the monkey bars."

And being good at something—anything—can help them build confidence and develop pride in themselves. Not being very good can have very negative consequences as Nathan, an 8-year-old with a disability, explains when he is asked by the interviewer "This boy doesn't really think he is very good at it [going on the monkey bars], so how do you think that would make him feel?" Nathan's response? "Sad and mad, and ashamed of himself."

Not all children become skilled easily. For those who struggle with basic playground skills, playground time can be uncomfortable and lonely. Naturally, children who lack movement competence, who are awkward or clumsy, do not take part as frequently in playground activity. They do not spend as much time engaging in vigorous activity that will benefit their hearts, lungs, and muscles. They may spend a lot of time alone or with younger children whose games are not as physically demanding. Thus it is important for a child to have competence in general playground activities, in handling play vehicles (e.g., tricycles and scooters), and in playing games if he or she is to be fully engaged on the playground.

# CONCLUSION

Children can get lots of moderate and vigorous activity on the playground if they take part in a range of games and activities. To take part fully, they have to be skilled. Children who possess the needed movement skills and knowledge of how to play can more easily enter playground activity and establish friend-ships that help them feel included. They may be better prepared to resist being bullied or intimidated and may even develop leadership skills that enable them to prevent such problems for others. On the other hand, children who lack movement skills may end up feeling lonely, sad, and even unhealthy because they have lost out on opportunities to play.

It is important that parents, teachers, and playground leaders learn to look closely at individual children to detect who is experiencing plenty of moder-ate to vigorous activity during playground time—and who is inactive. Intense activity during play is beneficial for everyone, and everyone should engage in it to reap these rewards. Sometimes a cursory glance at the playground leaves the overall impression that everyone is vigorously active. Since there is a lot of activity, it may *seem* as if everyone is busy playing *something*. Yet a closer look shows that there are children on every playground who are not active and who, in some cases, are completely isolated. Some may be sitting on the steps or passively watching the activity from the safety of the bicycle rack. Others may always be talking with a friend and avoiding movement, while still others may take every opportunity to hang onto the hand of the recreation supervisor or teacher. There can be many reasons that these children are not active, but the bottom line is that for them the wonderful potential of playground play is not being realized. Although this book was written for all children, the children who are inactive (but wish they could be active) and who are isolated (but wish they could join in) may benefit most from the application of this book's ideas.

# Understanding What Motivates Children to Participate on the Playground

To understand why a child does the things he does on the playground, and doesn't do other things, we need to understand his motives for participating in or disengaging from the play around him. When Sally goes to the playground she has a lot of potential choices: "[I can]…swing on a tire swing, slide down a slide, climb up a slide…climb up a ladder, climb on equipment, monorail or zip line, play tag, talk with friends …" Some of these choices are active social ones, while others are passive and solitary. What motivates a particular child to join and take part? Why might another child hold back or withdraw? The studies that have been done by our research group show that two factors seem to predict what children do on the playground. The first predictor is if they feel they are good at the skill or activity. The second predictor is if they value the skill or activity, if they think it is important for them to do for some reason. How do these two motivations develop in children, and what can parents and teachers do to influence them?

Joining in a playground activity is a personal choice. Although external factors can influence this decision, the choice to be active (or not) is made by each child for himself or herself. It's true that other children sometimes control who plays a game or has access to the slide and that a teacher may sometimes shoo kids out to the playing area for recess. Ultimately, however, each child is free to decide whether to participate actively. Once children reach age 4 or 5, no parent or instructor is right there to tell them what to do or when to do it. This freedom is, in fact, part of what makes free-play time so exciting for children.

Yet it's clear that plenty of children are choosing not to participate. To help kids become involved, educators and parents need to understand why they might choose not to do something that, for many, is inherently fun. In choosing whether to participate actively on the playground, girls and boys are motivated by their personal answers to two basic questions:

1. Do I want to do this activity?

2. Can I do this activity?

When a child answers yes to the first question, he is saying that he *values* the activity: "I want to do this because I like it, it's important, and it feels good!" When he answers yes to the second question, he is evaluating his own *competence*: "I know I can do this activity because I have done it before," or "because my mom says I can do it," or "because I am a big strong boy!" How can we ensure that when children ask themselves these questions, the answer to both is yes?

# DO I WANT TO DO THIS?

From the child's perspective, the main point of going to the playground or going out for a recess break at school is to have fun. Some activities (e.g., hanging upside down or going down a slide quickly) may be fun because of how they *feel*, while others may be enjoyable because of the excitement of chasing, evading, or even being caught. Many playground skills are intrinsically motivating because they give children such thrills. Another example is swinging, which can be even more interesting if the child throws his or her head way back so that the world looks upside down. Thus children may say, "I want to do this," because of the very exciting feelings they experience during playground activities.

> **"S**hellie, age 7, when asked why kids bounce balls: It's sometimes fun and you can really bounce it and sometimes you can bounce it as high as you can; you can bounce it when you're running and you can bounce it—so it's fun. You can do a lot of things just by bouncing it. **"**

Children may also choose to join an activity simply because they want to be with their friends; the activity itself may not be especially important to them. If their friends go to the swings, they go there too, and if their friends are hanging upside down on the monkey bars, they want to take part in that activity.

There may also be other, more complex reasons for children to do a specific skill or take part in a certain activity. For example, children may choose to do certain activities because they feel it is *important* to do so in light of their own age or gender—that is, doing the skill contributes to their feelings of self-worth. Skipping rope may be very important to a 9-year-old girl because she feels it is something that most girls her age are learning how to do; for a boy of the same age, however, skipping may hold very little importance. Shellie explains this a bit when she says "maybe you jump up and down and you see lots of other younger kids doing it, instead of the older kids, and you want to be like the older kids, cause you're an older kid."

So when a girl or boy asks, "Do I want to do this activity?" the answer might be "Yes, because it is fun and it feels good," or "Yes, my friends are doing it," or "Yes, I am in grade 3, so it is important for me to do this."

Other answers to the question may involve *costs* associated with doing—or not doing—a particular activity. Perceived costs are very important to children, even young ones, when they make decisions on the playground. In this context, the word *cost* refers to the negative aspects of doing or not doing a task. For example, running might make a child tired, constructing a snow fort might require the child to go back inside to get his or her mittens, hanging upside down might lead to a nasty fall, and going down the slide in a skirt might be uncomfortable to a child's thighs. In each case, the child is considering straightforward *physical* costs of doing a particular skill or activity.

Even more important, children may consider *psychological* costs of doing an activity. If a child doesn't run, he may not get out to the field in time to be picked for a team. If she tries to hang from her knees and falls, she may be embarrassed. A child who is clumsy or unskilled may be humiliated by peers' comments if he or she tries to participate. Imagine the humiliation involved in *not* being able to skip rope when the other girls are doing so, or in having no one pass you the ball because you always drop it. When a child is faced with this kind of potential outcome in participating, it is not surprising if he or she withdraws from the activity or avoids free play on the playground altogether.

So there might be any number of complex reasons a child might answer the question "Do I want to do it?" such as the following:

- Other kids my age do it.
- The other kids think it is important.
- It's fun.
- It feels good.
- I'll do it to be with my friends.
- It makes me tired. It hurts.
- If I don't do it, I will be teased.
- When I try to do it, the other kids laugh at me.

Despite any concerns that a child may have, the answer to the question "Do I want to do this?" must be yes if a child is to be motivated to join in on the playground. And there are many reasons that children naturally *want* to engage in play. But when we consider that the answer to the question may depend on the perceived costs of participating, or of not participating, it is clear that the answer to the second question, "*Can* I do this?" is also very important.

# CAN I DO THIS?

Being good at something really matters on the playground. In fact, being good at a task is the most frequent reason for doing it—and, according to the children in the studies that have been done at the University of Alberta, being good at something makes it fun. We all tend to experience satisfaction in doing things we are good at, and children tend to choose activities they are good at rather than ones that they cannot do well.

When children lack skill, the costs of participation may be too high. The child may be teased, taunted, and excluded. If Kwame is in grade 2 and playing tag is the major activity each day at recess, then he will need to be good at it. If he is slow, if he can't climb quickly

**"Terry, age 8, with a mild disability:** I like zip lines. I'm actually pretty good... [Y]ou know how people go, like they zip up and then they put their feet against the poles and bounce up. I can do that... I bounce back and then I can bounce back over here too... I'm good at zip lines... [B]ut I only do it when I can do it without my hands getting frostbite. **"**

enough to escape up the slide, or if he can't slide down the pole to avoid being tagged on the platform, then he may not want to be involved, even if all of his classmates are playing this game. In fact, if he perceives that he is not good enough at the game, his motivation to participate may be very low; thus, being "not good enough" carries the risk of exclusion.

How do kids know they can do a skill? When children are very young (i.e., less than 4 years old), simply *trying* to do a task is celebrated by the child and by parents. There is lots of clapping and excitement when baby takes those first steps, and this positive reinforcement likely convinces the child that, just by trying, he or she can do almost anything. The available evidence confirms this idea.

As children mature, however, the answer to the question "Can I do this skill?" is influenced by the belief that performance must meet certain standards. These are *perceived* standards for success; that is, they are constructed by each child based on what he values and how he interprets his experiences. For example, a girl who thinks she is really good at running might decline to enter a race because "a kid she knows runs even faster and she doesn't want to lose" (according to Emily, age 7). Her acceptable standard of performance (being the fastest) is high, and because she worries that she cannot meet it she chooses not to be involved.

Children in grades 2 to 4 seem to understand that taking part in certain activities can be embarrassing or unsatisfying if they cannot do well and thus their participation would be risky. Doing well can involve both excellent performance of a skill *and* understanding of the rules and strategies relevant to using the skill. This is particularly true for games such as soccer, American football, baseball, and common playground games such as tag. These games involve the risk that children will feel embarrassed if they perform badly (e.g., miss a shot or drop the ball) or feel stupid or silly if they do not know the rules or do not know what to do. For example, in her first exposure to freeze tag, Darlene thought that if a participant was caught, he or she had to stay still until the end of recess! She did not understand that another runner could "release" her from being frozen by crawling through her legs. She confided later that this misunderstanding made her feel stupid and that she had a hard time forgetting about her mistake. In this playground context, then, it was important to be able to perform the skills involved *and* to know the rules of the game. The perception that certain standards must be met in order for a child to contribute sufficiently to a group game can strongly influence both withdrawal (a personal decision) and exclusion (a decision made by other children).

The fact that there are standards to be met means that the playground is not the simple context we might think it is. In fact, it is a very important context for children—an important place for them to do well—because it makes the difference between being included and being isolated. The classroom is also an important context, of course, and being good at school subjects may be important in that setting, but being a good student does not necessarily influence one's social acceptance. On the playground, however, physical skill and social acceptance are strongly linked. This difference might derive from the fact that doing spelling or math is rarely a public act, while hanging upside down from (or falling from) the monkey bars, and catching (or missing) a fly ball can be seen by everyone. It might also be the case that catching a ball is simply a more highly valued activity in childhood than is doing well at math. So if someone is good at catching a ball, he or she gains social status, and people want to be friends with that person.

The playground, then, may be more important than the classroom. On the playground, everyone sees what you do (e.g., falling, dropping the ball), and, more important, they depend on your doing some things well when they play with you.

# AM I GOOD ENOUGH?

While being good at something is related to choosing to do it, *believing* that you are good or bad at it is just as critical. When a child believes that she is good at something, this belief depends on her interpretation of her success at using the specific skill. For example, a child can perceive himself to be very good at skating forward because he has done it successfully many times and at the same time think that he is very poor at skating backward because he fell and hurt himself the first time he tried it. The child's perceived competence in these two skills differs greatly, even though the skills themselves are related.

For most people, believing they are competent is based largely on whether they actually *are* competent and have witnessed the outcomes of their competence. These outcomes involve input from many sources—both internal and external. Feeling the satisfaction of completing a task may lead to feeling competent; receiving feedback from others may also contribute to perceived competence. For instance, parents may tell a child that he or she is good at something, and peers may cheer when the child scores a goal. Such feedback may go a long way toward encouraging the child to think that he or she is good at the task. The same effect may result simply from becoming competent in a skill quickly (after only a few practice trials).

Very young children tend to believe they will be good at new skills simply because they do tend to improve their skills so quickly. As they get older, though, they will use all kinds of more complex information to develop their beliefs about what they are (and are not) good at. They may consider how often they have failed as compared with how often they have succeeded. They may consider the information they get from others, the effort they put into doing a given task, how good they are in relation to peers, and their assessment of the difficulty of the task.

Research (our studies about playgrounds, as well as Jacqueline Eccles and Alan Wigfield's studies of motivation in the classroom) has demonstrated that perceptions of competence are important as early as the kindergarten year. Perceptions of competence determine the extent to which a child expects to be successful in using a skill and thus how he or she behaves with respect to that activity. When children are asking themselves "Can I do this task?" they consider how likely they are to be successful in meeting the expected standards.

They may consider how difficult the skill is for them to do. They may also consider how difficult the skill seems to be for their peers. Doing a flip around a horizontal bar may be considerably difficult for most children who are 6 years old yet rather easy for most children who are 10 or 11. A boy of 11 may think the flip around the horizontal bar is a relatively easy task for most children his age but still believe that it is hard for him to do. His perception of his personal competence may be influenced by how hard he thinks the task *should* be for someone his age. He might think, "All the other boys my age seem to be able to do this, but I don't think I am very good at it. It is hard for me to do this kind of flip." This belief may make him less likely to choose to attempt the flip.

It should be clear, then, that children's perceptions of their chance of success on a given task helps them answer the question of whether they can do the task. If a child is very young, he will expect to do well on most tasks regardless of whether this is actually so. If he is older, his standards for doing well may be more complex and may depend on perceptions of what is hard for him and what is hard for other boys his age. Thus, doing well may mean something different depending on age: Younger children may think that doing well means just getting the task done ("I did it"), whereas older children may measure the quality of their performance in relation to that of their peers ("I did it better than Joey").

Intuitively, it makes sense that children who really are less competent would believe themselves to be more and more incompetent as they age, especially if they see an increasing gap between their own skills and those of their peers. This appears to be the case for children with disabilities or awkwardness; it also might be true for many children who are not identified or labeled but who don't take part in playground activity as much as they might. When these children compare their own skill with that of their peers, they see the differences, and, as these differences grow, the children feel less and less competent—and less and less inclined to join in. Such perceptions may be reinforced by comments and other feedback (gestures, looks, actions) they get from friends, parents, and teachers.

"Trevor, age 8: Well, there's some—there's one person, James, and . . . he can't run very fast and he gets tagged, and then he just sits and sobs, "It's not fair! It's not fair! I always have to be It." . . . He gets tagged and he sits down there and sobs. . . . He just says, "No, I shouldn't have to be It because I am the worst person to be It."

When these kids have the choice to be actively engaged on the playground with their peers, they may think, *I'm not very good at this. I probably can't do it, so I'm not going to try to do it.* Their answer to the question "Can I do this?" is no, and that means that these particular children are likely to be left out and isolated if the activity is popular and valued on their playground. Not surprisingly, our research at the University of Alberta revealed a strong relationship between perceptions of low competence on a skill and choosing to avoid doing that skill.

One powerful motivation to participate on the playground is a child's desire to be with friends ("Do I want to do this?"). For many children, playing at recess involves just trying to stay with their friends and play, but this endeavor can be very difficult for children who do not have the skill they need to adequately take part in the activity—or who *think* they do not have the skill (i.e., whose perceived competence in the skill is low). The game of tag, in its many variations, is probably the most popular game on the playground. It can be played on a field, in the snow, in the water, or on a stairwell. It is meant to be fun. However, for children who do not have the skills to run fast, chase, dodge, jump down, climb up, or find strategies to avoid being It, tag can be a source of agony with a very high cost in the form of embarrassment, ridicule, and frustration.

# ENCOURAGING PARTICIPATION

The two best motivations for participating in playground activities, then, are for a child 1) to feel that he or she is good at doing things and 2) to value those things, to think that they are important or useful. How do these two motivations develop in children, and what can parents and teachers do to influence them? How can we ensure that when children ask themselves, "Do I want to do this?" and "Can I do this?" the answer to both questions is yes?

## Help Kids Develop Specific Skills for Typical Playground Activities

Again, thinking that you are good at something is the most important factor in determining whether you choose to do it. Perceptions of competence are widely agreed upon by experts to be at the very heart of motivation; thus, these perceptions are very important, and, because actual competence may be the basis for positive *perceptions* of competence, parents and teachers should do everything they can to help children become skilled. Telling kids that they are good at something even when they aren't just doesn't work. We need to provide situations where children can develop and demonstrate real competence in performing meaningful and moderately difficult skills.

For this reason, parents and teachers should find out what is considered important on a particular child's playground, then teach that child the exact skills needed in order to participate actively on *that* playground. The skills checklists included in this book identify the skills that children tend to use on playground equipment. If a child has a good repertoire of these skills for each piece of playground equipment, and if he or she can do the skills without assistance and in the middle of free play with other children, then he or she will have the building blocks for inclusion in play, games, and, eventually, sports in the schoolyard and neighborhood.

## Teach Basic Rules and Strategies

In addition to helping children develop performance skills, you should equip each child with knowledge of the basic rules and simple strategies of typical playground games. As chapter 9 demonstrates, learning the simple rules of tag games and understanding the movement strategies that make for success in these games give a child the knowledge to take part in playground games and, eventually, in sports.

## Communicate That You Value Physical Skill Without Comparing Children

Very young children might want to be good at things that their parents clearly value. If you think swimming is important, your children may well want to do it. If hitting a puck with a plastic stick gets rave reviews from Dad, then Jason may think he is good at it. But if Mom and Dad constantly compare their child negatively with other children, especially those of similar age or younger, the child may be hesitant to try new things and to practice skills. Letting children know that skill develops gradually, that practice and experience are important, and that making mistakes is an important part of learning how to do something may help improve their views about their own skills.

**Emily, age 8: I tried to play soccer and then they got really mad at me because I never played it and stuff, and I was making their team lose . . . so then they kicked me out of the game. . . . I just wanted to try it and they kicked me out because I wasn't good.**

## Keep Play Positive

Parents and teachers need to make sure that the play environment is not caustic for children. Name calling and teasing should not be tolerated. Memories of previous experiences may play a particularly important role in determining the value that a child places on doing a specific activity. If a child remembers feeling happy, satisfied, or proud (perhaps due to the reactions of people around him or her), then that activity may become increasingly important to the child. On the other hand, if the child remembers feeling foolish, humiliated, sad, or embarrassed, the activity is likely to decrease in value in the child's mind. Memories may be particularly powerful in movement activities where kids are subject to the (often harsh) scrutiny of their peers. Adults who were clumsy (or who believed they were) describe their childhood experiences in sport and physical activity as embarrassing, humiliating, frustrating, and disappointing. They remember feeling ashamed and stupid about being inept, and their response was often to withdraw from activities because of the high cost of showing what a "spaz" they were, even when they really wanted to join in and when their friends were involved. The emotional cost was simply too high. Withdrawal from participation, and the subsequent social isolation, are seen frequently in children with disability, children with movement difficulty, and other children who may not be clumsy or unskilled but may have cognitive or language deficits that interfere with their motivation. Thus, despite the stigma or cost of choosing not to participate, withdrawal can seem like the best choice available to some children.

Emotional costs may be particularly associated with contexts in which there is a high demand for exceptional movement competence, as in competitive games. Competitive contexts have long been associated with negative emotions in children's sport. The perception of a competitive motivational climate (discussed further in chapter 8) may play an important role in children's decisions to drop out or withdraw from full participation. Competitive contexts put pressure on children to demonstrate how good they are at something, or that they are better than their peers. Even activities that are primarily cooperative (e.g., building a snow fort, group skipping) require that each participant make capable contributions to the activity. During both competition and cooperation, being unable to contribute sufficiently will put the whole group at risk of losing or not finishing what they have started.

It may be for this reason that children with poor movement competence or disability tend to withdraw even from cooperative activity on the playground and spend more time alone. Negative memories of being teased, being viewed as "no good," being humiliated, or simply being unable to contribute to the group's goal may make children reluctant to join. It is essential that children be provided with positive emotional contexts for learning, practicing, and taking part in physical activity and playground activities.

### Explain the Benefits of Practice and Playground Skill

We may be able to influence the value of a skill by emphasizing or even exaggerating its importance to the child. This can be done by providing models, asking family members and friends to do the skill in order to show that they value it, and simply telling a child that it is important. For example, explaining that dodging and running fast are important in playing a social game like tag may encourage a child to practice dodging and running even though such practice requires temporarily tolerating the cost of running to the point of gasping!

If a child avoids an activity largely because he or she doesn't value it (e.g., feels that the physical cost is too high or doesn't see the activity's relevance), parents may want to try to increase the perceived value of the activity, either by showing excitement when they do it themselves or by explaining that doing it may lead to other benefits such as making friends. Parents might also want to explain that *not* trying the activity can lead to exclusion and isolation. Most important, parents may want to do everything they can to help their child become good at the activity; if the child is good at it, then he or she will value it.

### Provide Opportunities for Practice

Giving children a chance to privately practice skills that they're struggling with is a great way to help them get better at using those skills. I recall spending a few hours at the big curly slide to teach my 4-year-old son to go down it without the pressure of other children being there. Once he could do it with me there, he was able to join in the activity at his day care rather than stand at the bottom of the slide and cheer others who did it. Thus we might try "scaffolding" a task by giving direct assistance while a child is learning how to do it; we can also help by having the child try easier versions of it first (see chapter 6) and by adopting good principles of practice (see chapter 7). These instructional approaches may encourage children to produce new answers to the questions "Do I want to do this?" and "Can I do this?"

# CONCLUSION

Motivation is evident in a child's decision to do something active, to try hard once doing the activity, to keep trying the skill or activity when things go wrong, and to find ways to solve movement problems on the playground (e.g., choose strategies, get extra practice). Children's perceptions of themselves and of the value of doing activities are important predictors of their motivated behavior on the playground. Their participation choices are affected by their beliefs about themselves, their beliefs about the importance of an activity, their perceptions of the context in which they are about to be active, and their memories of earlier experiences with these activities. If any one of these factors appears to be sufficiently negative, a child may choose not to take part; in contrast, if the child feels positive about an activity's possibilities, he or she may happily choose to engage in it.

# Understanding Assessment

**B**eing competent at specific skills on the playground is extremely important for children. Skills determine what they can do—and with whom. Skill level may also underlie the beliefs that children hold about themselves, and these beliefs or perceptions influence many of the choices they make about taking part in activities and playing with friends. If there are children you care about, you probably want to know whether they have sufficient skills for the playground and how you can help them where needed. Thus you need to know how to assess their playground participation, as well as their ability to perform specific skills needed to take part in playground activities.

*Assessment* is merely a means of gathering information that contributes to our understanding of a person. Tools used for assessment can be quite diverse in form and can be administered in many different ways. An assessment does not necessarily rely only on data collected from just one test or one source. Parents, leaders, and teachers should use all of the information at their disposal. Your own observations, comments made by a child about his or her experience, things that other kids say about a child, and your knowledge of events from the child's past can all serve as good sources of information to use in trying to understand whether a child plays optimally on the playground. In addition, caring adults should not ignore their common sense when helping children. Good assessors use all available sources of information to make decisions about children.

## WHY ASSESS?

Assessments in physical activity settings can be done for many reasons, one of which is to identify children who might benefit from intervention. This process, referred to as *screening*, can even be undertaken (unobtrusively) by parents. Assessments can also be done in order to place children in groups or programs that are most suitable for them, and this process is called *placement*. For instance, we might want to assess kindergarten children's play patterns to determine whether they are ready to join elementary-age children on the playground at recess. Or we might want to know whether a preschooler is ready to take part in the physical play that typically happens in a certain community program. We might also want to know if a child needs to join a remedial instruction program (without yet knowing exactly what remediation might be required).

Assessment may also be done to indicate more specific aspects of intervention—that is, to *diagnose*. This kind of assessment is done in order to determine strengths, weaknesses, and type of intervention needed. Specifically, we might want to identify exactly which skills a child has (and does not have) in his or her repertoire in order to determine which skills he or she needs to learn.

In addition, assessments can be done to evaluate whether an intervention is progressing as intended—that is, whether it is producing the desired outcome. In some cases, such assessments are used to decide whether children have learned the expected skills through an instructional program. For example, we might need to know whether a child has learned to swim well enough to be allowed to go independently into the deep end of the pool.

The Let's Play! program is designed to help learners become skilled in playground activities. The program includes a *screening device* (called a *playmap*) to help caregivers assess a child's participation in playground activity and *diagnostic devices* (called *playlists*) to determine whether a child has a reasonable repertoire of specific skills to use in typical playground activities for his or her age. The playlists will help caregivers identify the skills on which intervention is needed. Both the playmap and the playlists can also be used to determine whether a child should be placed in programs that demand certain skills, and whether interventions (practice, instruction, free play) are effective in helping a child learn new skills and use them freely in play. These assessment devices have been studied and tested with many children between the ages of three and eight.

# ASSESSING PARTICIPATION

To begin to understand what is happening on the playground, we must first be able to accurately describe what children actually do. The early studies that led to this book included observations and descriptions of children's behavior on the playground. One particular study indicated that clumsy children, or children who are physically awkward, were less vigorously active on the playground at recess and were also more isolated. That is, they spent less time playing with peers and more time alone. A related study showed that the physically awkward children were also less efficiently engaged in practice during school physical education classes. These results, based on grouped and averaged data, were, of course, not unexpected.

Some key information, however, was missing. Although these findings accurately reflected the averages of the groups that were observed by trained observers, *some* children identified as awkward were fully engaged in playground activity, both socially and physically. At the same time, some non-awkward children were not taking part fully in the observed activities. The long-term goal of these studies was to help *all* children be physically active with their peers on the playground, both during

**"**Ismael, age 7, when asked why free play is fun: We can play on the slide. You can go into the park and you can get on the other slide. You can climb the rope or go down the rope. You can go—you can go on the swings. You can go on the tire. You can play tag….**"**

and outside of school hours. We needed a sensitive tool with which to measure individual participation and engagement that would work for all children, as well as a method of using the tool that would enable us to determine who was taking part in activities with peers and who was not.

How do children spend their time? Many assessment methods rely on observation without intervention, so that children's natural play behavior is not interrupted. Screening of children often requires that teachers simply observe, using some kind of checklist to note whether every child engages in the behaviors that are of interest. Information collected in this way can be useful but is not terribly exact; however, screening devices are intended to be "quick and dirty," giving just enough information to tell the assessor which children require further examination.

If we want a more exact picture of intensity of play, simple counting devices (e.g., pedometers) and more extravagant measuring instruments (e.g., accelerometers, heart monitors) can capture descriptive information about how vigorously active a child is being on the playground. Despite being more precise, however, these measures are also noticeably intrusive and may interfere with a child's natural choices or tempo of play. Furthermore, they may indicate whether kids are moving but not what they are doing. Thus these measures are not included as part of the Let's Play! program, but they may serve as sources of extra information for parents and teachers who want to know the intensity of activity on the playground.

Here are several reasons why the Let's Play! screening process provides a good way to assess participation:

• **It contains meaningful items.** The research team began by finding a way to determine what children *typically* do on playgrounds, then focused on finding a way of screening for children who were not taking part in playground activity in the way their peers were. We observed many children over a period of several years and compiled lists of the skills and activities that children typically performed on a variety of playgrounds and playground equipment. We constructed these lists from hours of observations on many different playgrounds because we wanted to develop a screening device that could be used in many contexts rather than only in standardized settings such as clinics or labs. Thus the items in the playmaps are meaningful activities that children typically engage in on the playground. One playmap is for younger children (3 to 5 years) while the other playmap is for older children (ages 6 to 8).

• **It is quick and easy to use.** Teachers and instructors do not have time to observe all of the children in their care while they are out on the playground. Thus we decided to use the children to help us gather information about what they were doing, but many of the children couldn't read the lists of skills! We wanted all of the children, including those who are young or who have mild disability, to be able to help teachers understand their engagement patterns at recess. As a result, we developed drawings of children doing the skills. Illustrations have been used successfully before to help children report their behavior or their perceptions, and the drawings we used were tested to make sure they communicated the same thing to all of the children who were reporting on their activity. We also tested the illustrations to make sure that children and teachers both understood them the same way.

• **It's fun!** We rely on children's help through a reporting activity that is fun to do. Children can engage in the self-reporting activity by simply circling the items they have done, or by using stickers and crayons to highlight or color in the activities they typically do when they have free time on the playground. The attractive illustrations capture the attention of children, even when they are using them repeatedly over several weeks.

• **It provides accurate information.** Self-reports have been used in many studies of physical exercise, and they have generally been found to be reasonably (though not 100 percent) accurate for children. We wanted to minimize two kinds of errors: reporting things that did not actually occur and failing to report things that did occur. We tested for these errors and found that children can report fairly accurately what they do on the playground. Observers can also report children's activity accurately and reliably by using the screening test we have developed. So observers agree with each other about what a particular child has done, and observers agree with the children's reports about what they have done.

• **It differentiates between children who are participating and those who are not.** The children's reports can be used to pick out those who are not doing what their peers are doing. These children, who may make up as much as 30 percent of a group, need to be assessed further. It will become clear after the next assessment step (diagnosis) that not *all* of these children need interventions on their playground skill repertoires. Some may be avoiding participation even though they are physically skilled. For these children it is not skill practice and instruction that they need but other approaches that might help them feel more comfortable taking part (see chapters 8 and 9). This is the point of screening: we want to identify children who *might* benefit from further assessment and intervention.

# ASSESSING SKILLS

The way in which people assess children's physical skills is determined to a large extent by their views on children's motor development. For example, for many years, people assumed that motor development was determined largely by genetic endowment. The unfolding of movement skills during childhood was thought to be little affected by personal experience or the environment (i.e., the context in which a child grew up). Stages of motor development were widely assumed to just happen. Every child was expected to go through these stages, and features of the stages were used as points of assessment and instruction in physical activity. In each skill children were expected to go through three to five stages in order to reach a "mature" pattern. In throwing, for example, it was assumed that in order to participate competently in throwing games or tasks, children had to progress toward and eventually acquire the mature pattern (stage 5) of the skill.

Such work was based in part on the major assumption that it didn't matter what the circumstances were when children tried to throw a ball. That is, if a child had reached stage 3 in throwing, then he or she should use stage 3 throws in all throwing activities in which he or she took part. In this view, new circumstances—such as different playmates, different instructional or performance contexts, or different feelings and perceptions—should not significantly change the child's throwing performance. The "emerged" pattern should be resistant to change.

In this paradigm, assessment of movement competence was normally done in clinical settings or under standardized conditions, rather than in the context of normal play such as the playground or gymnasium. The idea was that bare-bones clinical situations helped us assess the child's true or underlying stage of development and allowed for comparison with other children. This approach to the assessment of motor development remains widespread and is exemplified by the development of standardized assessment tools that are administered under tightly prescribed conditions. Thus certain assumptions about how children develop and acquire skill have led to standard practices of assessment that are now reflected in many motor-skill assessment protocols.

Meanwhile, other theorists have advanced the belief that individuals possess certain kinds and degrees of *ability*, which serves as a basis for, and influences, how they learn and perform movement skills. This assumption has led to the development of many tests of movement skill that consist of test items meant to reflect a particular ability. For instance, a test of the ability to balance might involve standing on one foot with the eyes closed for as long as possible; duration determines the score. A test of eye–hand coordination might involve throwing and catching a ball at the wall; the number of successful repetitions determines the score. Once again, because this model involves an assumption that abilities are part of the child and are relatively stable, movement skill assessment is done under standardized conditions for everyone, usually in clinical or at least highly structured settings designated by the test developer. Testing in this way has increased the reliability of results and made it easier to compare individuals on a specific test or item.

To a large extent, assumptions that there are *stages* or *abilities* that underlie children's motor development provide the basis for current published tests of movement competence and motor coordination. Almost without exception, these tools take the form of standardized, norm-based tests which require significant training of the assessor. They usually also require standard equipment and procedures (protocols) for the assessment of performance. The term *standardized* means that these tests are intended to be used in a very specific way (as designed and tested by each test's author) that is described in a manual or textbook. The term *norm-based* means that they have been tested with many children of various ages to see how the "average child" performs at each age. Thus when a new child is assessed, his or her performance can be compared with the expected or anticipated performance for that age.

In most current tests of movement skill, an adult conducts a clinical evaluation of a child's performance of motor skills, and he or she often bases the assessment on the child's accuracy or timing in performing the skill or on the child's use of certain ways of moving the arms, legs, and trunk. The child may be performing the skill in unfamiliar conditions, and the testing is seldom done under conditions that are like those in which the skills will ultimately be used in play or sport. Children also usually know that they are being tested. Since it is recognized that this knowledge may make them uncomfortable and thus lead them to perform or behave in ways that are not typical for them, every effort is made by the tester to put the child at ease.

Once completed, these tests may tell a teacher or other adult where the child stands in relation to his or her peers (i.e., below average, average, above average). These tests are often used to prescribe interventions and place children in advanced or remedial programs.

One weakness of these models is that they do not assess skills in typical environmental conditions (e.g., in the child's neighborhood or on school playground equipment). Nor do they assess what a child does when he or she has free choice. For example, a child who cannot, or does not, perform a prescribed jumping task well according to the criteria of a test may actually engage successfully in many types of modified jumping tasks with friends during recess on the school playground.

While appreciating the value brought to the field by the two approaches just described, this book uses a third approach which we might call *context-based* or *ecological*. The assumption underlying this approach to assessment of movement skill is that the context of an action influences whether and how the action is performed. In this view, children don't move through stages but instead respond in the context in which they find themselves, with a movement that solves the present problem. Thus, if a child is given a large ball and a large low target at which to throw it, he or she might hold the ball with both hands and toss it underhand into the target. The same child, given a small ball and a target located some distance away, might throw overhand and generate as much force as possible to accomplish the task. Different contexts, then, are assumed to enable different movement solutions.

> " Regina, age 7: If you play just by yourself you're pretty lonely. "

Adopted as a basis for assessment, this approach suggests that it is more important for children to participate in the activity in free play, or meet the activity goal—to do the skill in *some* fashion—than it is for them to have efficient, "mature," or proficient patterns of action (which might be demanded in other contexts). If we believe that context *affords*, or leads to, the performance of skills, then we have to agree that there is no "right" way to do things and that children can participate by using various movement actions so long as they have a skill to draw on that meets the requirements of the context. Thus we can expect movement skills to be performed differently in different circumstances, settings, or moods. In this light, we can try to help parents, teachers, and instructors conduct movement assessments that are relevant to the child's own contexts rather than to a clinical setting.

The context or ecological approach used in this book is based on the assumption that children acquire skills through specific practice and experience. In other words, motor development arises as a product of the growing child's interactions with the environment, not as a result of growth alone. Motor development usually proceeds as an increase in the range of skills a child has, as well as in the efficiency, depth, and proficiency of the child's skills. Put differently, as a child matures and gets more experience and practice, the breadth of the skill repertoire increases (he can do more things!) and the depth of skill increases (he can do things more skillfully and adapt the skills to varying and more complex contexts). To meet the demands of a range of contexts, children need a range of skills—a repertoire with which to succeed in varying circumstances.

The Let's Play! diagnostic devices (the playlists), then, are used to determine whether children have a flexible repertoire of skills to use in the space and on the equipment available on their own playgrounds. The assessment evaluates the child's skill repertoire (his or her capability in a wide range of skills)—not the stage of development or the ability. The Let's Play! playlists can be used by adults to help children expand their skill repertoire. Based on research involving children who lack skill, it can be assumed that an expanded repertoire will increase a child's likelihood of positive participation and inclusion in playground activity. The assessment does not rely on comparisons between children.

The following characteristics make the playlists a good diagnostic tool for parents, teachers, and instructors to use with children they care about:

- **The assessment measures whole skills.** It does not assess the exact form of the skill performance (i.e., exact movement of the limbs, amount of force used, timing, or sequence of movements). The point of the assessment is to find out what a particular child can and cannot do on his or her own playground. For example, can your child hang upside down from her hands and knees on the horizontal bar?

- **The assessment includes a complete inventory of the skills that can be used on children's playgrounds.** Getting a complete list of the skills that children use on the playground required several steps. Observational studies of many children on the playground were performed in order to observe the various things children did on each piece of equipment when they were given free play time. Then children were asked if they could show the observers any other (different) things they could do on the equipment that they hadn't done while playing freely. Next children were asked to describe other things that other children (older or younger) did on the equipment. Each skill thus identified was added to the list in order to generate a cumulative inventory. The full inventory was tested with many children and eventually only one or two new skills were found when the list was tested. The list appears to be quite complete!

Children in preschool and children (with and without disability) in grades 1 through 4 were observed by university students and professionals in physical activity who had developed an observational sensitivity to seeing and describing what children actually do on each piece of playground equipment. The children were observed on their own school or day-care playgrounds or on large municipal or community playgrounds where several types of each piece of equipment were available. On these larger playgrounds, some equipment was available in many different forms—for example, the "baby" swing, regular swing, horizontal tire swing, vertical tire swing, saucer swing, and sling swing.

The assessment items themselves were tested by checking whether each item represented a skill that children did on a particular piece of equipment (e.g., the swing), and each list had to contain all of the items that could be done on that piece of equipment. The observers made sure they were not missing relevant assessment items that children might perform. This approach is quite different from most test development procedures, wherein researchers are trying to find just a sample of items that represent a range of possibilities, and where only a very few skills are actually selected for the assessment. In the Let's Play! program the goal was to identify and test *all* of the items.

> " **K**enneth, age 8: You don't have to be good at something to like it...the main thing is just to have fun! "

- **The assessed skills are illustrated.** Each skill has been illustrated by a professional artist, and the illustrations have been tested to ensure that their meaning is interpreted consistently by children (including young ones who cannot yet read) and that they represent skills that children had described and could confirm were used on their playground. It is also intended that children use the illustrations to identify skills they *can* do—or ones they *want* to be able to do. Therefore, it was very important that children's interpretations of the illustrations were consistent. A small number of children of various ages (from 6 to 9) were taken to the playground and asked to demonstrate each skill; they looked at an illustration, identified the pictured movement skill, and then did it. There were virtually no misinterpretations. One quick look was all they seemed to need before they ran off and performed the task.

Another reason for illustrating the test items was to increase the consistency of communication between experts, adults, and children about playground skills. To check the illustrations' effectiveness in this area, we conducted interviews with adults, including elementary school teachers and parents of school-age children who had no background in the fields of physical activity or physical education. These interviews were used to ensure that the illustrations were sufficiently explicit and that these adults perceived them in the same way that the researchers did. The ultimate goal was to develop an assessment instrument based on these illustrations that would help parents and teachers assess playground skills on each piece of playground equipment.

Furthermore, the line illustrations of these movement solutions capture the essence of each movement skill without being overly prescriptive about the exact form or style in which it is done (e.g., amount of lean, degree of knee bend). In this way, each illustration is like an impression or abstract (rather than a detailed blueprint) that is representative of a range of movements that all have the same goal and function. Thus children can look at an illustration and know what the task is; they immediately recognize the task and claim either "Yes, I can do that!" or "No, I can't do that yet." More than 200 illustrations have been tested.

- **The assessment contains playground skills typical of children of different ages.** After visiting more than 50 schools in Canada and Europe to ensure that the playground equipment included in this book is typical, we can be assured that it is! Many years of testing with preschool children with and without disabilities in a variety of day cares confirm the appropriateness of the preschool items. A recent test of 30 schools indicated that the slides, swings, composite climbers, and other equipment featured here are like those located in schools in western Canada. Furthermore, during the developmental work and pilot testing on the playground skills in this book, children from 10 schools were involved in studies to develop the playlists. Finally, the playground skills were tested with a large number of children at a large school to ensure that they are relevant and to discover which are most typically done by children in each grade. About 150 school children were assessed on about 60 movement skills, and 40 day-care children were assessed on the preschool items. Skills were organized into subsets and sequenced according to how many children were able to do them independently. Movement skills that were done by 90 percent of the children in a certain grade, and by fewer students in the next lower grade, were identified as typical for the higher grade. For example, if 90 percent of the children in grade 1 could go down the slide headfirst but only 40 percent of the students in kindergarten could do so, then going down headfirst was identified as a grade 1 skill. The firm cutoff of 90 percent signifies that these may be essential skills for children in that grade. Children who lack these skills may be excluded from play because their repertoire is not sufficient to allow them to play freely with their peers. Many children who are in a grade below may also be able to do these skills, but more than 10 percent of that group can't do them, so we can assume that children can still take part with their peers in the lower grade without these skills. There may be many other skills that a majority of the students in a particular grade can do simply because skill repertoires may vary from context to context. In summary, the grade listings are simply for guidance in prioritizing skills to be learned by all children where the appropriate equipment exists.

In the final testing of the skills, one or two tasks proved to be too difficult, a few were too easy, and a few that appeared legitimate to the testers were not allowed on the school playground (for example, some classrooms had rules against going down the slide headfirst) and so were not observed in that setting. Some of these tasks have been retained in light of evidence that a few children do them on their local playground when not constrained by school rules. These tasks are presented as advanced skills for children who need an exceptional challenge in their playground skill repertoire.

# CONCLUSION

It can be difficult to design and develop a screening process and an assessment tool for use by parents, teachers, and recreation instructors in real, everyday circumstances. The approach taken by the research team at the University of

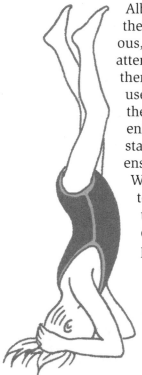

Alberta to develop the Let's Play! playmap and playlists was to identify the activities that are common on playgrounds and discover the numerous, varied skills that children at different grade levels perform. Rather than attempt to describe these movements in words and sentences, we illustrated them so that they are easy for both adults and children to understand and use. We employed a process for testing that included checking to see that the items were clear and made sense to children and adults. This approach enabled us to be confident that children can look at the drawings, understand the indicated movement, and try to reproduce it. We also checked to ensure that adults can use the illustrations to assess children's movement. We used small, repeated steps that give us confidence that the screening technique is fun to use, that it identifies children who may need help, that the test items represent authentic skills used in the everyday lives of children on playgrounds, and that the items can be tested right on the playground by people who have an interest in play but are not experts.

# Using the Playmap to Assess Participation

Jane Watkinson
Nancy Cavaliere

**A**re you a parent who wants to know if your child is playing vigorously with other kids on the playground? Are you a teacher who is concerned about the social interaction of that shy little girl in your class? Do you want to know if a child is taking part in the same activities as other boys his age?

This chapter walks you through a process that uses free play and a tool called the playmap to help you assess children's participation on the playground. By using this process, you will obtain accurate information about which children are taking part sufficiently to gain the benefits of free play. The process is efficient; it helps you get information quickly and easily—both about and from children—so you can determine whether a particular child needs further assessment.

## THE PLAYMAP

The playmap is a visual tool designed to allow easy reporting of the activities in which children are taking part during their time on the playground, whether in a school setting at recess, in a preschool or day-care setting, or during other free-play times at or near home. A specific version has been developed for use with preschool children and another for use with school-age children (see figures 4.1 and 4.2); either version may be printed from the CD-ROM that accompanies this book.

Each playmap contains illustrations of the activities that are typically done on playgrounds and in outdoor play spaces by children. Children and adults alike can use these illustrations as a reference point for reporting the playground activities in which children choose to participate. It's as simple as giving the children an opportunity to play, guiding them through the process of indicating their play activities on their personal playmap, and then comparing the playmaps to get an idea of who's doing what.

Since playgrounds are much the same wherever you go, each playmap's illustrations of playground activities will be applicable in your specific playground. Differences may exist, of course, in the amount or newness of equipment, but there are plenty of playground commonalities. Most playgrounds, for instance, have slides and climbers of some sort (often "composite" climbers with vertical ladders, horizontal single and parallel bars of differing heights, bridges, poles, cargo nets and other equipment that fosters various kinds of activity); for safety reasons, climbers are normally surrounded by sand or another

My name is: _____

# What did you do today?

Chase

Climb small equipment

Do gymnastics

Play with small toys

Play on tire swing

Tricycles

Dance

Balance

Play on bars

Wheels

Strike balls

Jump

Hang from ropes and bars

Wagons

Catch and throw

Run

Play on slide

Play with friend

Play in snow or sand

Play on swing

Watch other kids

Play on climber

Play with balls

**Figure 4.1** The preschool playmap: What did you do today?

My name is: _____

I am in grade: _____

# What did you do on the playground today?

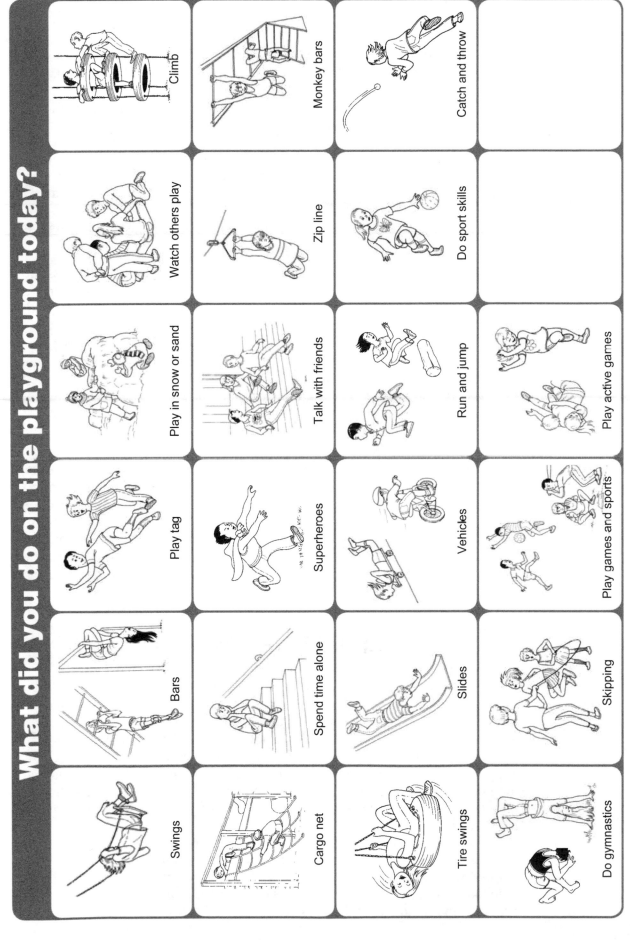

**Figure 4.2** The school-age playmap: What did you do on the playground today?

Adapted, by permission, from E.J. Watkinson et al., 2001, "Engagement in playground activities as a criterion for diagnosing developmental coordination disorder," *Adapted Physical Activity Quarterly* 18: 18-34.

soft surface. In some locations swings are no longer available on playgrounds, though they are a standard feature of most school playgrounds in Canada and the United States and throughout Europe.

Each playmap's illustrations reflect standard playground equipment, and what is pictured may or may not be *exactly* what is available on the playground of the children to be assessed. This is fine. The activity itself is important. Use the items on the playmap that approximate the equipment available at the child's local playground. The critical issue is to assess children on their local playground in order to find out whether they have the skills to be safely active on that particular playground.

Using a playmap to discover who is, and who is not, engaged in activity is a two-step process:

1. **Find out what the majority of children are doing.** There are almost no universally done playground skills. What is typical depends on the play context and on the group of children who are playing. Activities that are popular with the children from one classroom may not be done (or be highly valued) by children from another classroom at the same school and even at the same grade level. Some activities are, however, quite common on the playground, meaning that groups of children in each classroom typically do them, and the first step in analyzing the children's self-reports is to identify the common activities for the group. The playmap contains meaningful and accurate assessment items for most North American playgrounds and thus it can be used in various contexts, just as it was during the test development process.

2. **Compare each child's individual report with the common activities for his or her group.** Children who are not doing activities that their (classroom) peers are doing may be isolated and inactive. According to observations done during the testing phase of these reports almost 30 percent of the children in each class can have profiles that appear to be problematic! Although this proportion may seem quite high, a screening device should err on the positive side of detection in order to be sure that it identifies all children who might have a problem rather than miss some who do.

# SELF-REPORT METHOD

Teachers and recreation leaders do not have time to watch and record what every child does, so the playmap offers a way to let the children report on their own activity. This method has been tested and used throughout our research program. It provides excellent and accurate information about children's play patterns and can be used accurately with children in grades 1 through 3. (For children in kindergarten, a combination of observation and self-report is recommended because the reliability of self-reports about free play by children at that age has not been tested. Instructions for using this method are given on page 39 in this chapter.)

The self-report assessment process starts with a period of free play. Children are allowed to spend 10 to 20 minutes on the playground engaged in activities of their own choosing. The children are then gathered into a classroom or other quiet area where each child fills out his or her individual playmap to report the activities that he or she did during free play.

Children should be told how to report the kinds of activities they do. They need an adult to go through the playmap with them, slowly at first, to make sure that they know what is being asked of them. Immediately following the free-play period, have the children settle in at their desks or another location where they will be able to hear and write comfortably. Each child needs a playmap and a writing utensil; the playmaps can be printed from the CD-ROM that accompanies this book. This activity can be varied by using stickers instead of check marks.

Have the children write their name and grade at the top of the playmap, then ask them to put down their pencils and listen to the instructions before going any further. The following script can be used with the children.

We are going to learn about the kinds of things that you did on the playground today. The first thing I want everyone to do is close your eyes. Now, think about the [recess or play period, as appropriate] that we just had. Try to remember the different things that you did at [recess or playtime]. Maybe you played a game or used the playground equipment or maybe you did something else. Keep your eyes closed as you think about the kinds of things you did this morning. [Allow 20 seconds.]

Okay, boys and girls, now you can open your eyes. In front of you is a playmap. You can see that there are lots of pictures of children doing different kinds of play activities. What you are going to do today is circle the activities that you did at [recess or play time]. I am not talking about yesterday or last week. I only want to know about the kinds of things you just did. So, if there is an activity that you just did at recess, you are going to [circle it or put a sticker on it]. If there is a picture of something you didn't do at recess this morning, then you are going to draw an X on it.

Don't start yet, because there are a few things that are really important to remember while we are doing this activity. The first is that it is important not to make things up! It doesn't matter if you did lots of things or only a few things. The most important thing is to be honest and to circle only the things that you just did at [recess or play time]. Whatever you did is okay. It isn't a contest or a test. It is good to work on your own, though, because I want to know what each of you did. Now some of these pictures may not look exactly like what you did, but if they are pretty close and you think it is *kind of like* what you did, then you can circle them. It also doesn't matter if the pictures are of boys or girls. This is about the activity.

To ensure that children understand the task, it is helpful to ask some follow-up questions. The answers provided by the children provide a basis on which the teacher, recreation leader, or parent can then provide clarification as appropriate.

Now, just to check that everyone knows what we are supposed to do, I am going to ask you some questions:

- Do I want you to circle [or put a sticker by] the activities that you did yesterday?

- Do I want you to circle *only* pictures of things you just did at [recess or playtime]?
- Does it matter how many pictures you circle?
- Is it important to be honest?
- Can you circle a picture that is pretty close to something you did, even though it isn't exactly like it?

Once confident that the children understand the task, the adult can lead them through the playmap one picture at a time.

Let's begin with the picture of the girl on the swing. Can everyone find that picture? Now, think about the recess we just had. Did you play on the swings? If you did play on the swings, then please [circle or put a sticker on] the picture of the girl on the swing. If you did not play on the swings, then please put an X over the picture. Remember, circle [or put a sticker on] only the things that you did at [recess or play time] today. Let's do the next one. This is a picture of . . .

The last item on the playmap gives children a chance to include anything else they did that was not captured in one of the pictures. Here, they can either draw a simple illustration or print the name of the activity (e.g., "I played house")—or both. It is important to guide the children through the playmap each time it is filled out. Although some children will not need this support the next time and may work ahead, other children will need continued guidance.

# INTERPRETING THE RESULTS

The teacher or leader should gather the playmaps for all children in the group and analyze them together. This process takes only a few minutes. The first step is to determine which play activities are most socially relevant for the group, and this information can be tabulated on a blank self-report form. For example, if five children circled "played on the swing," then five check marks should be made for that item on the blank form. Thus the instructor simply notes the total number of children who chose each item on the playmap, and the results indicate which activities were done by a sizable portion of the group (say, 25 percent) and therefore can be considered to have social relevance for the group. Typically, a group of children will report doing five to eight activities during a 15-minute play period.

The next step is to ensure that each child in the group engages in a sufficient number of these common activities to be generally included in playground participation. Each child's report should be compared with the group report, and children who are not taking part in the common activities should be considered for further assessment. In a group of 25 children, this may mean that only 5 children will need further assessment, though more children can be assessed if you want additional information. Otherwise, the assessment is completed when it is clear that each child can engage in the activities that are socially relevant for the group. That is, if a child is participating in a reasonable number of activities that are commonly done by children in his or her age or peer group, then it is likely that no further assessment is required.

Let's consider some examples of assessment scenarios.

• A group of 7-year-olds who regularly come to the playground for arts and crafts programs also spends free time each day on the playground. The children's self-reports on the playmap indicate that their favorite activities are playing on the bar, playing on the curly slide, and running (i.e., chasing). However, the report for one child, Hart, indicates that his most common activities are playing on the straight slide and watching others play. The playground instructor should respond by using the playlists (see chapter 5) to test Hart's skills on the bar, on the curly slide, and in running in order to determine whether skill deficits might be playing a part in his decision not to participate in the group's typical activities.

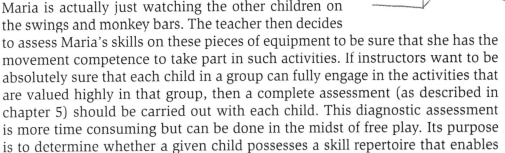

• An instructor who suspects that a child may not be reliably reporting his or her activity can use the same checklist to carry out an observation; the instructor may also decide to further assess the child. For example, a playmap completed by a child named Maria indicates that she plays on the swings and monkey bars with her classmates. Her teacher is aware, however, that Maria is shy and usually spends her time alone in class, so she conducts a short observation of a play period and finds that Maria is actually just watching the other children on the swings and monkey bars. The teacher then decides to assess Maria's skills on these pieces of equipment to be sure that she has the movement competence to take part in such activities. If instructors want to be absolutely sure that each child in a group can fully engage in the activities that are valued highly in that group, then a complete assessment (as described in chapter 5) should be carried out with each child. This diagnostic assessment is more time consuming but can be done in the midst of free play. Its purpose is to determine whether a given child possesses a skill repertoire that enables him or her to take part in the common activities of the playground.

• Letitia teaches a small class of students who have mild developmental disabilities. Their playmaps indicate that the group generally favors playing on the straight slide at recess; they also run and play with the balls. To ensure that each child in the class has the competence to be (and feel) included in these activities, Letitia can conduct a full competence assessment for each child in the class (see chapter 5); she can assess skills needed for running, catching and throwing, and using the straight slide. These assessments can be done in a group during a structured play time.

• Robert has a class of children in grade 1. He sends home report cards about their progress in reading, writing, and arithmetic, and he wants to include their recess activity in the reports. He can do so by sending home each child's playmap report, along with skill checklists from the playlists (playmaps and playlists can be customized and printed from the CD-ROM that accompanies this book). If the children in his class play on the swings, for example, Robert can attach a copy of the swing skills list to each child's report. He may even want to assess each child on these skills so that parents know exactly what their child can and cannot do on the swing (see figure 4.3 for a sample recess report card).

# Report Card

Student: _____ Class: _____ Teacher: _____

These are the activities _Timmy_ does most often at recess:

Here are some other activities he could practice at home:

These are the skills we will work on in physical education class next semester:

**Figure 4.3**  Sample recess report card.

# OBSERVATION METHOD

Although the tested use of the playmap is the self-report method just described, it has also been used as an observation tool by parents, teachers, recreation leaders, therapists, and others. In fact, watching a child and recording what he or she does may be a useful way for you to get information about the child you care about. It may be the only way to get information about what preschool children do!

One observer can observe more than one child during a play period. In research studies, observers often monitor several children at once by sampling the activities of each observed child. They do so by watching each child for 5 or 10 seconds and recording what that child does before moving on to the next child. Using this strategy, they may be able to observe four or five children during a recess period of approximately 15 minutes. If this is the case, then all the children in a class of twenty can be observed by a team of four observers during one play period. This ratio may be quite manageable in a day-care or preschool setting. In an older class where the teacher to student ratio is smaller, it may require observation over several play periods to get the same information. Conducting repeated observation periods (say, two or three 15-minute periods) strengthens the interpretations made on the basis of observation.

Another strategy involves watching one piece of playground equipment at a time and noting on the playmap which children are busy and involved at that piece of equipment. Observations of a given piece of equipment should be about 2 or 3 minutes long; the observer then moves to another piece of equipment, and so on, until each play space has been observed (e.g., slides, swings, ladders, climbers, open space). Using this observation strategy, observers might miss a child here or there as that child moves from equipment to equipment, but over the course of more than one observation period (i.e., recess or play period) such errors will be reduced. Observers need at least a 15-minute window of observational time in order to get a good picture of the typical activities in which children are engaging, and, again, the observation should be repeated several times before interpretations are made.

To use the observation method of playmap assessment, observers begin by familiarizing themselves with the playmap and practicing the use of it. This approach allows them to record information efficiently and accurately. During the observation itself, it is crucial to be discreet. Children may be told that the parent, teacher, or playground leader will be watching and learning about what kids do at playtime, but this fact should not be highlighted. Keeping at a distance maximizes the chance that children continue to play naturally.

In conducting a child-based (versus equipment-based) observation, the observer simply watches the child and records the activities that the child participates in by circling the observed activities. It does not matter how many times a child performs an activity or for how long—only that she or he actually did it. The pictures are intended to capture what children do; they are not intended as exact representations, and the observer should circle the activity that best conveys the idea of the observed activity. If a child takes part in an activity that was not represented on the playmap, that activity should be added to the playmap by hand, either in words or stick figures. If the observer is using the equipment-based method, then he or she simply notes on the playmap the names of the children engaged on that piece of equipment.

The playmap can be used to assess an individual child at play (that is, not in a group play context), but in this case the observer does not gain information about what the child's peers might be able to do. That is, the parent, leader, or teacher can only answer the question "What does this child choose to do when alone on the playground?" With this information, the observer may be able to identify activities that the child prefers and activities that the child is able to do, and the observer may then choose to introduce the child to other activities not currently being engaged in. Parents, for instance, may want to assess whether their child can do sufficient activities on the playground to be comfortable in a play group. In this case, the parents want to know if their child exhibits a repertoire or range of activities that he or she can do at the playground. For example, can the child play on the slide when the parent isn't helping?

Observing only one child, however, provides no information about whether the child is doing what his or her friends typically do on the playground—or even what this child may or may not do when playing in a peer group on the playground. For this reason, we recommend that the child *and* his or her peers be observed, if at all possible. We recognize, however, that there may be times when a parent or therapist is able to observe only the one child of interest (perhaps a child who is suspected of not playing with friends at school, or a child who is very young and not yet involved in play groups or school groups with other children of similar age).

Here is a summary of the steps to follow when observing an individual child:

1. Examine each illustration provided on the Let's Play! playmap so that you know what to look for.

2. Stand in an inconspicuous place and take note of the equipment on the child's playground. If some of the illustrations feature equipment (e.g., slides, climbers) that are not available on this particular playground, cross them out.

3. Watch only the one child of interest for this observation and move slowly around the play area in order to keep the child under observation at all times without being intrusive. Circle the illustration that best represents each activity the child does. For example, if the child is going down the slide, circle the sliding illustration even if the child is going down the slide differently than is depicted in the picture. Identify pieces of equipment that the child avoids.

# INTERPRETING OBSERVATIONS OF A SINGLE CHILD

Let's consider two potential scenarios for interpreting results after assessing one child.

• It is apparent that the child spends time actively on each piece of available equipment. The child likely has a reasonably good skill repertoire for handling playground activity. It is not possible to determine whether the child engages in the same activities as his or her peers, but it is likely that no intervention is required. Opportunities for continued play should be provided.

• In observations of another child, it is apparent that the child spends all of his or her free time on only two pieces of playground equipment and avoids other pieces of equipment entirely. It would be worth determining whether this limited range simply reflects the child's preference or whether he or she lacks the skills required for interacting with the other pieces of small and large equipment. The strategies for further assessment described in chapter 5 should be used for evaluating the child's ability to use the pieces of equipment that he or she has avoided during this observation. This follow-up allows the parent or instructor to determine whether the child has the movement competence to play on those pieces of equipment. The broader and deeper the child's movement repertoire, the more likely it is that he or she will be able to fully engage in unstructured playground activity when the opportunity is available.

# CONCLUSION

The Let's Play! program and playmap enable a simple process for gathering children's self-reports and identifying the favorite options among children in a particular group. Adults can use children's playmap reports to identify those children who may be at risk of being unable to do the activities favored by their peers. These children should be further assessed by using the methods described in chapter 5.

Teachers of preschool children (and parents of a particular preschool child) can use the self-report playmaps in combination with observations to see if a child takes part in activities on all of the available playground equipment. If not, further assessment should follow.

Using these methods also enables teachers, therapists, and recreation leaders to gather information that can be sent home to parents in the form of reports about children's playground engagement. When used in concert with the assessment tools presented in chapter 5, these tools can be used to help teachers inform parents about the skills that their children can and cannot do, and families can then use trips to the playground to foster skill development in children who lack sufficient expertise to participate gainfully in their peer group.

# Using the Playlists to Assess Skills

**5**

**H**ow do we know whether a child has the skills that he or she needs in order to use each piece of playground equipment? We know that children do not have to be experts, or outstanding athletes, in order to be completely involved in playground activity in the community or at school. They do, however, need to possess a skill repertoire that is sufficient for participating in play settings; more specifically, they need to know that they can do the skills required for participation on *their* playground.

It can be daunting to consider how one might assess a child on all of the playground skills that he or she might use or need. Each type of playground equipment (e.g., climbers, swings, bars, poles) gives children the opportunity to use many different skills. When you watch children on the playground, it is clear that they don't limit themselves, for example, to just climbing the ladder to the slide and going down the slide in a sitting position with their feet extended in front of them. In fact, there are times when this technique is the only one *not* being used by children as they scramble about the slide!

During our lengthy research program, we observed many children at play for many hours and discovered and categorized the skills that are most frequently used on each standard piece of playground equipment by children in the age range of 3 to 8 years. These skills form the basis of the playlists, which are the tools recommended as a follow-up for children whose playmap screening (see chapter 4) reveals a need for further assessment. (Complete playlists are provided on the book's CD-ROM.) The playlists help adults determine the skill repertoire of a particular child. The assessor's role is to determine whether a child can do a particular skill, as well as the conditions under which the skill can be done; this information facilitates the ensuing instructional process.

This seemingly daunting assessment process is made manageable by the illustrated playlists, which are easy to use. Like the playmap, they use generic illustrations to depict skills that you may observe being used by the child you are assessing. As you can see from the sample shown in figure 5.1, the playlists illustrate many skills for each piece of equipment: the swings, slide, bars, ladders, balls, ropes and so on. Children do many different things on or with each kind of equipment. Unlike some adult exercise equipment, playground equipment invites various actions, and children find new things to do there all the time. Don't be put off by the number of playlists; you will not necessarily

# Bars

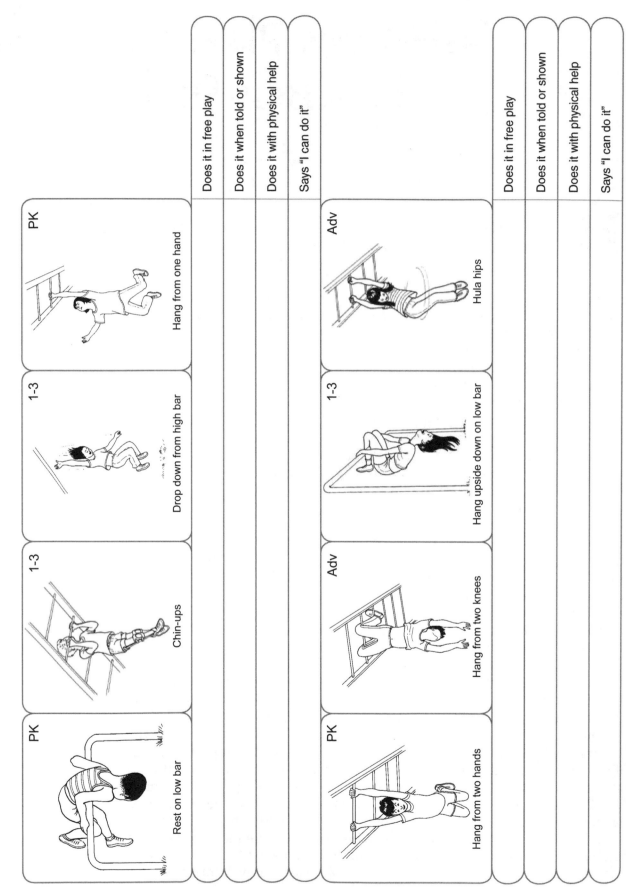

| | Does it in free play | Does it when told or shown | Does it with physical help | Says "I can do it" |
| --- | --- | --- | --- | --- |

**PK** Hang from one hand
**1-3** Drop down from high bar
**1-3** Chin-ups
**PK** Rest on low bar

| | Does it in free play | Does it when told or shown | Does it with physical help | Says "I can do it" |
| --- | --- | --- | --- | --- |

**Adv** Hula hips
**1-3** Hang upside down on low bar
**Adv** Hang from two knees
**PK** Hang from two hands

**Figure 5.1**  Playlist sample: Can you play on the bars?

Reprinted from E.J. Watkinson and J. Causgrove Dunn 2003. Applying Ecological Task Analysis to the assessment of playground skills. In *Adapted physical activity*, edited by R. Steadward, G. Wheeler, and E.J. Watkinson (Edmonton, Alberta: University of Alberta Press).

use all of them. You will start with the skills (identified through the playmap screening process) that you know are valued on this particular child's playground.

The playlists offer many advantages as a tool that you can use to help a child develop movement competence. They can

- be used by people who are not movement experts;
- be used in the real-life environmental conditions that are most important and familiar to the child;
- help teachers, leaders, and parents make good decisions about what to teach;
- be used in normal, everyday circumstances without interruption of play;
- provide accurate and useful information about what children can and cannot do; and
- be used with children of almost any skill level and experience level.

Using the playlists to assess specific skills involves five basic steps:

1. Decide which activities are going to be assessed (e.g., swinging, climbing, bouncing balls).
2. Get the playlists for the activities you want to assess and study the skills that are included there.
3. Determine which skills in the activity checklist are already part of the child's repertoire; some of these skills will become evident during free play.
4. Use prompts to determine whether the child can do the remaining skills—and how much help the child needs in order to do them.
5. Decide what to teach after conducting the assessment.

# STEP 1: CHOOSE THE ACTIVITIES OR EQUIPMENT TO ASSESS

The playmaps discussed in chapter 4 include a number of activities that have been identified as common on playgrounds. Let's now imagine that you are an instructor who has used the screening playmap to determine that eight activities are typically done by the children in your group. Imagine as well that you have identified two children who are not taking part and that you are now ready to begin your assessment of those two children on the eight activities or pieces of equipment most typically used by children in their group. You will be assessing these two children, then, on the skills that every child in the group must have in order to take part fully in this particular group's free play. You may limit your assessment to these eight activities only.

At the preschool level, assessment should be done on all of the activities that are included on the preschool playmap, and eventually also on the activities that are also typical for kindergarten children on the playground. The preschool playmap identifies 14 activities, including playing with balls, playing on the swings, playing on the slide, and playing with vehicles or tricycles. If there are swings or climbers, then the adult should use the playmap to determine whether everyone is able to play on the swings and climbers. Before doing the more thorough playlist assessment described in this chapter, then, the parent or instructor should first know whether a particular child participates on each piece of apparatus on his or her playground. If the child spends no time on certain pieces of equipment, then these pieces should also be fully assessed.

If you haven't screened at all, or if you have observed only one child in play, then you are free to start almost anywhere. Start with one piece of equipment, perhaps one that the child chooses, and then do the pieces of equipment that the child seems to avoid. Your task is to determine this particular child's overall playground skill repertoire.

# STEP 2: GET THE PLAYLISTS FOR THE ACTIVITIES YOU WANT TO ASSESS AND STUDY THE SKILLS THAT ARE INCLUDED THERE

The playlists are located on the CD-ROM. Each playlist indicates the typical grade levels at which each skill is typically acquired. Coding is as follows: PK indicates preschool and kindergarten, and 1–3 indicates grades 1 to 3. Advanced skills (A) are those that not every child is likely to be able to do, even in grade 3 or with physical help. These "extreme" skills (e.g., going down a slide on your feet with no hands, hanging upside down from your knees on the monkey bars, kicking an airborne ball) are complex and pose good challenges for skillful children.

Each playlist also provides room for new skills to be added. If there is an unlisted skill that children do on the playground in question, then that skill should be added and described (whether in words or in a drawing) so that other children on the same playground can be assessed on that skill if it is a popular one. For example, on one playground in Edmonton, Alberta, girls in grades 1 through 3 hook their knees over a low horizontal bar, with their hands gripping the bar between their knees. Next, they spin 360 degrees around the bar, sometimes with the help of a push from a partner but sometimes generating the momentum themselves by sitting on the bar and then suddenly dropping forward or backward to start the rotation. This movement solution for playing on a horizontal bar is not seen elsewhere in the city. It is a local custom, but one that is so common on that playground that every child there should learn it.

# STEP 3: DETERMINE THE CHILD'S CURRENT SKILL REPERTOIRE USING THE PLAYLISTS FOR THE ACTIVITIES YOU HAVE CHOSEN

Look through the relevant playlist skills so that you have a good idea of the various skills children may exhibit when using a piece of equipment. For the slide, for instance, the playlist illustrates quite a number of relevant skills. Take time at the start to let the child play freely on the slide so that you can check off any skills that he or she initiates in that list when engaged in free play there.

To do this, you can simply wait near the slide and see if the child does anything on it during free play. If you do not have enough time for this approach, you might simply lead the child to the equipment (e.g., the slide) or limit the child's choices so that the slide is an obvious pick—for example, by taking the child to the playground but not bringing along a ball, tricycle, or other piece of attractive equipment. With a younger child, you may be able to make the slide more interesting simply by standing near the bottom of it. You can then ask the child what he or she can do on the slide.

Children will respond to this invitation in various ways. One child may slide down feet first, whereas another goes head first. Each child will choose based on several considerations: the nature of the environment (Is the slide high? Is it slippery? Is there a big drop to the ground at the bottom? Are lots of kids lined up and waiting?), the nature of his or her own experience (Has the child done this before? Does the child think that he or she *can* do it?), and the nature of the skill itself (Is it hard or dangerous?). In other words, the child will decide what is best for himself or herself, and the specific skill chosen (e.g., sliding headfirst, sliding feet first) will be the outcome of this decision process.

To record information about the child's skill repertoire, put a check mark beside every skill in the slide checklist that the child does by himself or herself in free play. These are skills that you no longer need to worry about—if a child spontaneously does a skill when entirely free to choose his or her activities, then you can have some confidence that the skill is firmly entrenched in the child's skill repertoire. You know that the child can do the skill without assistance.

When using this approach, you will check-mark a skill if you think the child has done it reasonably well—that is, well enough to use it in the midst of free play with peers. The important thing is whether the child can use this skill effectively in his or her real world. For example, say that you are watching Emily on the swings at her school playground. It is not important to know whether she swings harder and higher than other children or whether she leans more or swings her legs faster than normal. The point is this: Does she meet her goal of swinging? Does it look like swinging to you? That is the question.

This focus differs quite a bit from that of most assessment devices for movement skill, wherein testers typically want to know how well a particular child does on standard equipment as compared with the norm for other children. But with the playlists you are looking to see if the key elements or key features of the skill are present, *not* whether the child does each part of the skill exactly as other children do. For example, a child may pump a swing by leaning back and straightening the knees during the forward motion of the swing, then bending the knees and leaning the trunk forward when the swing moves backward. These aspects (or features or elements) of the movement skill may be virtually the same for each child, but the *amount* of lean, the *speed* of knee extension and bending, and the *height* of the swing (based partly on the length of the ropes that hold it) will vary between children and between playgrounds. Thus, when you use the playlists to assess children's skills, you have to make a judgment about whether the child's skill is *sufficient*—sufficient for playing with others, sufficient for playing alone, and sufficient in the eyes of his or her peers.

# STEP 4: USE PROMPTS TO DETERMINE WHICH SKILLS NEED WORK

Having developed a good idea of which skills the child's repertoire already includes, you can now use prompts to see what other skills he or she might be able to do with some help. (Prompts are discussed in greater detail in chapter 6.)

- **Verbal prompt.** When the child does not take advantage of the opportunity to demonstrate skills during free play, you can simply ask, "Can you use the slide? What can you do on the slide? Can you show me what you can do on the slide?" The child can then demonstrate which skills are included in his or her repertoire. The child can choose, for example, how to go down the slide, how fast to go, and even whether to go up or down the slide. If you want to know about ball skills, you can simply ask the child to throw a ball. The child can choose the distance from the target, the kind of throw to use, and even the size of the ball. Give each child plenty of turns! Once again, if a child can demonstrate a skill simply when asked, then it is quite likely that this skill has been very well learned; thus it is unlikely that the child needs instructional help with it.

- **Visual prompt.** If the child does not respond, you can show the child the playlist of skills for that activity and ask which skills he or she can do. Then, if the child wishes, he or she can show you. This form of demonstration gives the child free choice between all skill options; thus it may be more motivating than a demonstration performed by an expert (e.g., the instructor or a skilled child). Showing the illustrations to the child is a way to present him or her with a choice of movement solutions for the activity. This is a very different testing approach from the usual one, wherein the assessor gives a perfect demonstration of the expected response and wants the child to mimic it as closely as possible. Because we are interested in learning which skills are in the child's repertoire, we want to know which solutions can be produced by the child *independently*. Put check marks on the playlist beside all skills that the child shows you when he or she sees the illustrations.

- **Physical prompt.** If the child is not able to do the illustrated skills, you can select a particular skill and help the child with physical support as he or she does the task. Check marks in this column of the playlist indicate that the child is not able to produce the movement independently in play and thus that these particular skills should serve as a focus of instruction. You can use physical help for any or all of the remaining skills on the playlist for your activity (sliding) so that you have a thorough idea of exactly what the child can and cannot do by himself or herself on that particular piece of equipment (the slide) or that particular activity (catching a ball).

# STEP 5: CHOOSE SKILLS TO TEACH

Instructors should choose only one or two new skills at a time for a particular child. The adult can then help or encourage the child in a focused way each time they are at the playground; once a focus item has been learned, it can be check-marked on the child's playlist, and instruction can move on to something else (if needed). Concentrating on more than two skills is too difficult for both the child and the adult; it can cause free play to be interrupted too frequently for instruction. Once a child starts to learn a new skill, it is important to provide plenty of time for practicing it in independent play.

You may be able to increase the child's motivation by asking what skills he or she wants to learn; you can use the illustrations to have the child pick out a few skills that he or she would like to be able to do. As much as possible, the playlists are organized according to task difficulty, and children can be encouraged to learn easier skills first, then move on to those that are common for their age group and particular setting. This is not, however, absolutely required. We do not know for sure that competence in one of these skills is a prerequisite for doing another. They are all simply things that children do.

# CONCLUSION

The playlist offers an effective means of finding out exactly what a child can and cannot do that would enable full participation in play with peers. Adults should assess the skills that are most relevant for the child—whether because a certain piece of equipment is available on the child's playground; because peers in the group play frequently on that equipment; or because the child shows an interest in a particular activity or piece of equipment by watching it, staying near it, or spending time on it. The assessor should first determine whether the child can demonstrate movement solutions on his or her own during free play. Then, if needed, the assessor can use verbal, visual, and physical prompts to find out whether the child can do the task when asked to do it or when shown the playlist, or whether the child needs physical support in order to complete the skill. Finally, let the child choose one or two new tasks to learn.

# Teaching Playground Skill

Instructors and parents often give physical, visual, and verbal input to children who are trying to learn new skills. The adults might hold the children, move their arms and legs, or support their body weight at the same time that they are gesturing, demonstrating, and giving verbal instructions for doing the skill. Thus a lot of information comes very quickly to the child, who meanwhile is trying to concentrate on the *doing* of the task.

The model of instruction described in this chapter takes a different approach. Its basic premise is that instructors should give the minimal amount of help required for the child to do the skill. In this way, the child is as independent as possible each time that he or she tries to do something on the playground.

The basic teaching model described in figure 6.1 helps you identify exactly what aspects of the skill the child can do without some form of assistance. For example, perhaps Henry can reach for and grip the bar when he sees it but cannot lift his legs to get them off the ground. Or perhaps he can hang easily with his feet off the ground if someone helps him get his hands over the bar with his thumbs in the correct position. In this model, the key to effective—but not excessive—teaching is to give the child every opportunity to be as independent as possible in doing a task. She may, for instance, need help only at the very beginning of the task, after which she can complete it alone. The major principles of this direct instruction model are to give only the help that is required in order for the child to reach the movement goal; to withdraw your help appropriately, safely, and gradually; and to ensure that the child has many, many practice trials (not forced, but encouraged) for a skill that he or she is trying to learn.

## DIRECT INSTRUCTION MODEL

*Direct instruction* means that the instructor and the student have a goal in mind and that the instructor provides specific instructions and feedback geared toward reaching that goal. In using *indirect instruction*, on the other hand, the teacher poses problems or questions, thus guiding learners to find solutions to movement problems. Both methods of instruction are useful for teaching playground skills.

Models of direct teaching for movement skills have been shown over many years to improve movement competence, and they have been used across the

## Environmental Prompts

Provide the opportunity and the appropriate equipment for the child/task interaction.

*Is there anything I can do to the physical or social environment, without saying anything, touching, or supporting the child, that will make this task easier?*

## Verbal Prompts

Use general or specific verbal cues to draw attention to some part of the task or to cue the child to a particular action at a particular time.

*Without saying too much, what are the most important words to describe the action needed here?*

## Visual Prompts

Use gestures, partial demonstrations, or full demonstrations to draw the child's attention to critical aspects of the performance.

*What specific body actions am I trying to communicate, and how can I do so?*

## Physical Prompts

Provide minimal physical guidance, partial physical support or even complete physical manipulation to help the child understand what the basic actions of the skill are and to support task completion.

*What specific body actions am I trying to communicate, and how can I do so?*

**Figure 6.1** The direct instruction model is based on increasingly intrusive prompts. At each point, you are seeking to answer the question "How much help should I give?"

Reprinted from E.J. Watkinson and A.E. Wall, 1982, The *PREP program: A preschool play program for moderately mentally retarded children* (Ottawa, Canada: Canadian Association for Health Physical Education and Recreation). By permission of E.J. Watkinson.

spectrum of learners, from elite performers to those who have difficulty acquiring simple skills. The model involves using systematic prompts or supports that come from the environment or the instructor. Some prompts are very unobtrusive, such as simply taking a child to an apparatus and allowing him or her to explore skills on his or her own. This approach may result, for example, in a child trying to climb a ladder to a slide and sit at the top or simply swing around a support pole. Other prompts are quite intrusive, such as choosing a skill for a child, explaining the skill, demonstrating the skill, lifting the child and putting him or her into a position that enables performance of the skill, and physically supporting him or her throughout the performance of the skill.

The direct model described in this chapter includes four levels of prompts or teacher assistance. In the first level, the teacher uses a more indirect approach, acting on the environment rather than on the child. The three other methods or levels of instruction are increasingly direct in that the instructor has a very structured idea of what he or she is trying to teach, provides specific sequenced instruction, and gives feedback on how well the child has matched the teacher's instructions.

# ENVIRONMENTAL PROMPTS

This first, and least intrusive, level of assistance is a natural one in which the instructor does not give verbal directions or physical help but tries to set up or select the environment that most suits the needs of the child in performing the task at hand. The instructor might also modify the environment (e.g., move or change the size or shape of equipment) in order to make the skill, or some approximation of it, possible. Such arrangements may help make the goal clear to the child. Bruner (1983) described this approach as *reducing the degrees of freedom of the task*, meaning that the many factors that have to be considered or handled in doing the skill are simplified and thus made more manageable for the learner. For example, a rolling ball involves fewer degrees of freedom (i.e., unpredictable aspects) for the learner to deal with because its path and speed are more predictable than those of a ball that is thrown. When you "trap" a rolling ball, you at least know that it will be at ground level. With a thrown ball, in contrast, the catcher needs to know how high or low the flight path is, as well as how far to the left or right, how fast the ball is moving, and even how much spin the ball was thrown with!

Others have used the term *environmental design* for this kind of instructional assistance. In teaching jumping, for example, a teacher may get a child to jump farther and higher by providing physical obstacles or even imaginary barriers. We could also refer to this approach as providing the optimal amount of challenge. On the playground, a parent can show the child that a bar just higher than the child's head may be the best one for hanging and swinging (lower bars make the action too difficult, and of course out-of-reach bars make it impossible). Similarly, a lower platform (at knee height rather than hip height) may provide an easier launch point for jumping than would a more demanding (higher) physical structure.

The point here is that the adult makes relevant aspects of the environment clear to the child and may even shape the environment so that the child is more likely to be successful. For example, the instructor or parent can provide the child with a ball of appropriate size (e.g., a small, textured ball for an overhand throw; a larger, softer, lighter ball for the novice catcher) or with appropriate structures for initial attempts at a skill before the child tries it in a more demanding environment. Examples of environmental prompts can be found in figure 6.2.

If this instructional level works, the instructor may encourage (or simply allow) the child to practice using this environmental challenge. In this case, the instructor can be very unobtrusive, and this kind of teaching can even be used while the child is in the midst of free play with other children. Practicing

## Environmental prompts

- Are not intrusive
- Do not interrupt play
- Allow a child to do the skill independently

## Examples

- Offer a small ball rather than a big ball to a child who is throwing
- Offer a volleyball to a learner who is trying to throw a basketball into a basket that is high
- Take the child to a hip-height horizontal bar to practice rolls around the bar
- Hold the swing still while the child gets to a standing position
- Keep other children away from the horizontal ladder when a child is slow at trying to grasp each rung
- On a bike: put pedals into the optimal position (with one pedal up, but just in front of vertical) to generate force for the first push

**Figure 6.2**   Characteristics and examples of environmental prompts.

alone (i.e., without the instructor's help) is much easier for the child if the equipment is the right size—such as a ball that fits nicely in the child's hand (i.e., is correct for his or her size) or a properly sized bicycle that maximizes the child's chance of being successful.

Teachers and parents make some of these environmental adjustments naturally. They may, for example, keep other children at the bottom of the ladder while a timid child climbs, or they might temporarily direct other children to go elsewhere so that the child in question has the time he or she needs in order to try the task. When children are first learning to use a spiral slide, they can be intimidated by bigger or more capable children who are impatient and anxious to go first, who brush past the more timid child at the top of the slide, or who make comments and noises that might distract the child. Controlling some of these environmental factors may be all a child needs in order to get the practice trials necessary for learning a new skill.

These approaches are helpful because they give the child time to try the skill without other children making it more difficult, yet the child actually does most of the skill himself! A good rule of thumb is that the more independent practice attempts the child has (with no external help from an adult), the sooner she will gain the skill, speed, and confidence to use the skill on the playground when other children are around.

Thus the following is a good first question for the instructor who is trying to help a child do a new skill: *Is there anything I can do to the physical or social environment—without saying anything or touching or supporting the child—that will make this task easier?*

# VERBAL PROMPTS

The second level of instructor prompts involves verbal instruction to help the child understand the skill and its critical features (see figure 6.3). This kind of instruction can be given through general suggestions or questions (e.g., "Can you try to do this faster?") or through very specific suggestions about how to move the body (e.g., "Use both hands at the same time" or "You have to keep your leg straight to do this"). Bruner (1983) suggested that the teacher could signal important features of the skill to the child as a method of instruction. For children with intellectual disabilities, verbal prompts should be very direct and objective, rather than strategic or detailed.

Before using verbal prompts, the instructor should think about the skill's *key features*. What makes this skill (e.g., throwing, catching, sliding, hanging, swinging) what it is? What are the important movements in performing the skill? Where do one's hands and feet go? What is the starting position? How does one land?

Finding the right words may take some experience. For instance, in trying to teach a child to pump the swing, using the word *pump* may not help, because even for children who know the word it tends to make them think of bending and straightening their legs. The key feature of the movement, however—the one that really provides the force to move the swing—is leaning back at the start of the swing phase and leaning forward during the recovery phase. So an instructor should say, "Lean back now," or "Get ready to lean forward," as appropriate, just before a phase starts, thus giving the child a chance to adjust his or her posture. At this level of assistance, the key question the instructor should consider is "Without saying too much, what are the most important words for describing the action needed here?"

It is not always easy to identify the key features of a skill, but the illustrations provided in the playlists can help instructors see the most critical aspects of each skill. Children themselves can sometimes extract these key features by looking at the illustrations, and instructors who feel confident that they understand what it takes to do the task can help by pointing out these features.

---

## Verbal Prompts

- Offer direction while minimizing intrusion in play
- Allow a child to learn to cue himself

## Examples

- Catching: "Use 'quiet hands' to catch the ball."
- Batting: "Swing the bat flat."
- Jumping down: "Can you land on your feet without making any noise?"
- Slide: "Try sliding feetfirst before headfirst!"

---

**Figure 6.3**   Characteristics and examples of verbal prompts.

It is important to understand that knowledge of key features can be very basic or quite sophisticated. For example, a child may declare that he or she needs to step forward when throwing a ball (a technique that the child has observed), whereas an adult instructor might understand that what is needed is a weight shift in the direction of the throw, which can be accomplished in part through the step forward, but also by adding up the forces that are produced by trunk flexion, forward hip rotation, *and* stepping forward if they are done at the right time.

# VISUAL PROMPTS

The third level of prompting involves gestures, demonstrations, or partial demonstrations—in other words, visual prompts (figure 6.4). Bandura (1986) and Bruner (1983) both supported the notion of helping learners acquire knowledge about complex motor skills by giving them the opportunity to observe good models. Such prompts are usually coupled with verbal prompts to bring the child's attention to key features that need particular attention or specific actions that need to be changed or eliminated. For example, "Try it like this, Janice, so that both of your knees are tucked up to your chest" (and the instructor brings one knee up to his or her chest to show what is meant). Or "Watch the way Sean keeps his hands on the rails when he slides."

Demonstrations can be used effectively in a variety of ways. Sometimes a child just needs a starting point or general idea of the skill, and demonstrations can be done primarily to provide a broad idea rather than the details. In other words, it may be better only to show—rather than show *and* tell—the child

## Visual Prompts
- Can be used for more than one child at a time
- Can be used without verbal interruption to play (but usually will need verbal prompt as well)
- Allow the child to do the skill more independently
- Can be full demonstrations or only partial cues or gestures

## Examples
- Give a full, but slow demonstration of the skill: "Watch me do it slowly."
- Stop the demonstration at a critical place: "See what happens when I get to this position? I bend my knees and tuck my feet up through the bars."
- Demonstrate the movement of only one limb. "Your knee should bend this much"; "Your hands should be here."
- Point out a good demonstrator: "See how that boy swings himself way back?"

**Figure 6.4**  Characteristics and examples of visual prompts.

what to do! Learners need time to watch a good demonstration and extract the key aspects of the performance themselves, and distracting them with verbal instructions at the same time may lead to information overload.

At other times, demonstration can be used to illustrate a specific detail (e.g., angle of knee bend) or a technique (e.g., a certain grip). When a demonstration is being done in order to make such specific corrections to a movement, or to give information about special features of the task, it is critical to draw attention to the relevant movement or body part. If the instructor simply demonstrates the whole task, the child may not notice how tightly tucked the knees should be or exactly where the hands should be placed, or the child may be looking at the knees when the instructor really wants her to focus on the hands. Thus the instructor should ask, "What specific body actions am I trying to communicate, and how am I going to do so?"

# PHYSICAL PROMPTS

The fourth and most intrusive kind of prompt is the physical prompt (figure 6.5), and it should be used as little as possible. Physical assistance can be minimal (e.g., catching the child at the bottom of the slide) or substantial (e.g., supporting the full body weight while the child slides down the pole). Because giving physical assistance makes the child entirely dependent on the instructor to accomplish the skill, it should be used selectively and withdrawn as soon as reasonably possible. The instructor might start by providing complete physical

## Physical Prompts

- Are intrusive
- Make the child dependent on the instructor
- Should be reduced as soon as possible

## Examples

- Complete physical assistance: Sit on swing and pull child onto lap to swing together.
- Complete physical assistance: Put hands around child's hips and lift her up to the bar, then put your hands on top of the child's to ensure a strong grasp of the bar.
- Partial physical assistance: Put hands on child's hips to slow descent down cargo net.
- Partial physical assistance: Hold seat of bicycle to keep it upright while child pedals.
- Minimal physical assistance: Run beside bike and touch seat from time to time to reduce swerving.
- Minimal physical assistance: Guide child's foot to next rung as she climbs down a ladder.

**Figure 6.5**  Characteristics and examples of physical prompts.

assistance—for example, helping the child on and off the equipment and supporting the child while he or she is there—and then fade it out as soon as possible so that the child is being supported less and less. For instance, the instructor can start by lifting the child up to the monkey bars and letting the child hang for increasingly longer times on his or her own while the instructor simultaneously increases the amount of weight the child supports compared to the instructor. Next, the instructor can fade back to merely prompting the child to reach and jump up for the bar while the instructor gives a little lifting push at take-off, quickly letting go when the grip is firm so that the child is doing the maximum amount of physical work for himself or herself.

Physical assistance can also be restricted to use at only the beginning or end of the skill performance. For example, if the child is trying to shinny up a pole, the instructor might either let him go as far as he can and then support him while he gets up to the top, or support him at the bottom of the pole and let him do increasingly more work by himself as he gets near the top. The two keys here are for the instructor to give no more physical assistance than the child needs in order to reach the task goal or do the skill, and for the instructor to reduce the assistance given in a systematic fashion so that the child becomes more and more independent in performing the skill.

The instructor should always keep in mind that if the child requires physical assistance to complete the task, then she is entirely dependent on the helper for every single practice trial. Since people need dozens, if not hundreds, of practice trials in order to get good at a skill, the process is more efficient if practice trials can be initiated and performed entirely by the child.

Also, consider that the presence of physical prompts often alters the skill itself. A child does not have to perform the same force-absorption movements (e.g., bending the knees and hips) when landing in an adult's arms that she must do when landing on her own. Thus, unless the catching support is withdrawn as soon as possible, the child will not have learned safe landing techniques. Physical support should not be withdrawn abruptly; it should be withdrawn as soon as possible in a gradual way. When you are using physical prompts or physical assistance of any kind, ask yourself, "Am I letting this child do as much of the action as he possibly can, or am I supporting him more than he really needs?"

# USING PROMPTS AND DIRECT INSTRUCTION

Instructors should see whether the child can perform the task based on the least intrusive prompts before using the next level of prompt when they start teaching. In other words, physical assistance should be used only when absolutely necessary. Whereas verbal and visual prompts can be given from some distance—and in the middle of group activity—without interrupting play, physical assistance requires the full attention of the instructor and disrupts the natural activity around the child.

Some experts suggest that children should be encouraged to solve their movement "problem" rather than be given intrusive help in the form of demonstrations, physical assistance, or even verbal directions. This raises a question that individual teachers have to answer for themselves. There are good theoretical reasons for giving a child time to figure things out and find a good movement solution, and there may be equally compelling social reasons for giving a child some well-thought-out instructional attention. Children may also show preferences for various methods of instructional assistance.

Many children will learn to use all the playground equipment in their neighborhood spontaneously, whether by observing others or by experimenting during play, but some may need to start with a good deal of physical assistance and then work toward independent performance over a period of time or over the course of several turns. For example, Andy, who was attending a kindergarten birthday party at a local playground, spent most of his time at the bottom of the big curly slide, laughing and clapping when his friends came down it in a heap. When asked why *he* didn't go down the slide, he said that when he climbed the ladder to the top "my brain told me not to go down." He could already go down smaller slides and straight slides, but no amount of verbal persuasion or verbal prompting was going to teach him to do the curly slide. No movement solution was evident to Andy—yet.

To help him get comfortable with the speed and curves of the slide, an adult began going down with him. In other words, she was providing complete physical assistance. For most adults, the inclination is to sit at the top with the child between the legs and then go down together, but this approach makes it hard to reduce the physical assistance you provide. A better method is to sit in *front* of the child and go down together with the child's feet pushing against your back (this is still a form of complete physical assistance, because you can slow the ride and prevent the child from falling off at the bottom). With your presence in front, the child will feel safe all the way down but will still get the feeling—and experience the thrill—of the trip! Once the child has gone down the slide a few times in this way, the adult can start down the slide and stop or slow down about 5 feet (1.5 m) away from the child. The child lets go of the sides of the slide at the top and begins to move down, but is slowed down by contact with the adult as they travel together to the bottom. As the child comes to feel more independent, the adult can stop farther and farther down the slide, and before long the child is going down the whole slide alone and meeting up with the adult's back only at the bottom. In Andy's case, it took only three such trips to the big curly slide before he was independently enjoying that piece of equipment. A thoughtful instructor can bring about significant changes in only a few minutes of concentrated assistance.

Children can go up and down a slide in many ways; learning to go down on one's bum is just the beginning. Children go down slides on their knees and feet. They go headfirst (with their hands out in front to break the landing) and feetfirst. They go on their backs and on their fronts. They climb *up* the slide in just as many different ways. However, the first essential skill is usually to slide down, and with this skill any child can take part in much of the playground activity on the slide.

The same sort of fading of physical assistance can help children gain confidence on other pieces of equipment, including bars (single or double horizontal bars at any height), ladders, and monkey bars (horizontal ladder). The key is to allow the child to be as physically independent as possible on each turn. When you are teaching a child how to hang on to a bar, your assistance can be in the form of supporting some of the child's weight from below (at the hips). When the skills involve swinging or twisting, rolling around the bar, or even turning upside down while holding on with the hands, it is a good rule of thumb to put pressure on the child's hands to help him or her hold on rather than supporting all the weight from below (e.g., by supporting the suspended legs or the trunk). Pressure on the hands can be reduced as the child gets better or stronger, but during the practice period this approach allows the child to really understand the nature of the task goal (in which a firm grip is needed in order to support body weight).

When children are trying to learn flips and inverted skills, the adult can keep firm pressure on one hand, to make sure that the child doesn't let go of the bar, while using the other hand to gently guide the feet or legs through whatever movement is required. For instance, a child who is learning to hang from a low bar with feet up but under the bar (see the illustration in the playlist of hanging from hands upside down) must first be able to hang on his or her own. Once that is achieved, the adult can put one hand over the child's hand around the bar to make sure that he or she holds on tight, then gently lift the child's bottom so that the child can bend the knees and tuck the shins and feet under the bar. Keep pressure on the hand on the bar, rather than on the child's bottom, and let the child hang in that position before adding more support to the child's bottom again to help the child uncurl.

" Cerie, age 8: Try it and try it, try it and maybe you get a bit better. Try it. "

## TEACHING BALL SKILLS

It is much more difficult to use physical assistance to teach ball skills. Somehow it just doesn't seem to help much for children to have an adult standing behind and putting the child's hands on a big ball that comes toward the child in an arc. It is more effective to use environmental prompts—that is, provide the best kind of ball for a given skill, modify the environment so that it is conducive to success, and modify the activity and the challenge of the task from time to time in order to maintain the child's enthusiasm for practice.

It is not easy to work on catching and throwing skills at the same time. Catching is much easier with larger, lighter balls, whereas throwing is easier with smaller balls that fit easily into the hand. While accuracy is required if you want your partner to be able to *catch* the ball, throwing can be practiced by itself with little regard for accuracy. That is, children can throw balls hard and far without worrying about whether they hit a target. If they have to throw for another child to catch the ball, the task is quite a different one. Begin catching with balls that are large (i.e., the width of the child's chest) and very light—but not so light that they are easily blown away by the wind. Light Nerf balls and other sponge products are okay, but because they are so light they tend to float in somewhat unpredictable ways. Balls also need to have enough heft or substance to be felt when they are contacted; otherwise this activity is only a timing skill—and a difficult one. If your hands are not in the right position at exactly the right time, the very light ball will bounce off of them into the air (try this yourself with a balloon or beach ball). Soft balls are, however, unlikely to hurt at all if they are mistakenly tossed into the face or bounced up too high on the chest. They are also fun to play with, especially indoors, but they are less likely to help a child become skillful in ball activities. Soft balls should be kept on hand, for sure, but lots of different balls should be available at all times.

## Catching

Catching activities can start very early in life. Children can sit on the floor with legs apart and receive a big, soft ball that is rolled gently toward the child (between the legs). Smaller balls can also be used and can even be bounced off of one leg to hit the other. The more times kids see balls bouncing, rebounding, or flying through the air, the more knowledge they gain about ball flight and trajectory for use in the future. The skill of anticipating where a ball will go after it leaves someone's hands or comes off a hockey stick, baseball bat, tennis racket, or table tennis paddle is critical if one is to take part skillfully in such games. A participant must know where to move to intercept the ball, or where to place a racket or paddle to hit a ball that bounces off a horizontal surface. In games that take place inside of four walls (e.g., racquetball, squash), one must also be able to anticipate where the ball will be after it rebounds off of two or more vertical surfaces (i.e., walls). Children and youth acquire this knowledge implicitly through experience with many examples (though knowing about angles of reflection can also be helpful). Thus an instructor's or parent's job is to make sure that a child has many practice trials with many different examples.

To practice catching, then, it is best to begin with lightweight but firm round balls that move in predictable patterns when bounced or tossed. Balls that are rolled on the floor to a child are more predictable in time and space than ones that are tossed or bounced, but all of these deliveries should be experienced hundreds of times as a child learns to deal with incoming balls. Bounce the lightweight ball so that it rebounds toward the chest for the early learner. Bounce it to the left and to the right of the child (alert them first if they need warning!) in order to get the child to move a little to intercept the ball. Once the child demonstrates some degree of skill, bounce the ball short and bounce it long (i.e., too close to the child), so that she or he learns to move forward, backward, and sideways to reach the ball (if catching) or avoid it (if dodging). Toss the ball high above your head and let it bounce one or two times before the child tries to catch it. Stand about 10 feet (3 m) from a wall and toss the ball toward the wall at chest height so that it rebounds toward the child, who is standing ready to catch it a few feet away from you. Use a light ball that won't hurt if it is missed, and bounce it high enough off the wall that the child has time to see it and react to where it *will* be.

When tossing a ball to a child for catching, toss it lightly with a gentle arc; if the arc is too flat or too high, the child may have difficulty in tracking it. Change the toss each time, making it a little higher or lower, flatter or more arced, harder or softer, as the child learns the skill. Bigger, lighter balls are easier to catch because there is more room for error in the placement of the hands. Eventually, you can toss smaller balls to the child, toss at greater speeds, and have balls bounce across unpredictable surfaces (e.g., lawns) and at different distances from where the child stands, so that he or she has to move faster and farther to intercept the ball. And remember that nothing is harder to catch than a ball thrown too fast from too short a distance. To coordinate a successful interception, the brain needs time to process the flight of the ball and make decisions about where to move the body and how to place the hands. Remember that this practice should be challenging but also enjoyable. If success is compromised too much when trajectories and speeds are altered, then the instructor can revert to more catchable tosses for a while.

## *Throwing*

Use variable experiences in helping your child learn to throw. Throwing can include passing a big ball (a skill used in quite a few team games, including basketball and rugby) to a target (e.g., person, net, basket). This is quite a different skill from throwing a ball a long distance toward a target, a task usually performed in a one-handed, overhand pattern with a small ball that fits easily in the hand. In helping a child practice throwing for distance, do not worry about a target at first. Throws that are forceful or cover great distance can be made more accurate later. For now, just have the child throw the ball hard and have someone (the thrower, a partner, or even the family dog) fetch it. The more children are encouraged to throw hard (use expressions like "Whip it!" or "Drill it!" rather than "Toss it" or "Throw it"), the more likely they are to develop a pattern of throwing that starts with their arm held way back and their opposite foot forward; they are also more likely to use timing lags at the shoulder and elbow to allow force production, as well as a whole-body effort that moves them forward towards the direction of the throw.

Balls travel farther if thrown with some—but not too much—arc. When throwing to someone fairly close, the child can use a trajectory that takes the ball slightly above horizontal. When throwing for maximum distance, the child can aim to release the ball so that it travels at an angle of about 45 degrees in relation to the ground. To get variability into the practice, you can ask for high balls, low balls, and grounders.

### Passing

In practicing passing, remind the child to make sure that the receiver is a comfortable distance away so that the pass is not a complete surprise; in addition, if the receiver is moving, then the pass must be thrown ahead of him or her so that the ball goes to wherever the receiver will be if he or she keeps moving (e.g., a step or two ahead—or more, if the receiver is far away). Of course, this activity also encourages receivers to keep moving once they get "open." If children can learn this skill, then they can become good partners in cooperative throwing activities, as well as in formal games. The same principles apply whether you are throwing or passing a ball to a partner, kicking a ball to a partner, or volleying a ball to a partner. The ball is sent ahead of the moving receiver. It doesn't hurt to explain this aspect of passing to the learner explicitly rather than waiting until he or she figures it out; some concepts can be explained to make a difference for a child, whereas others can be acquired simply through many practice trials.

# CONCLUSION

Parents and teachers can use a variety of instructional strategies to help children learn playground skills. The key is to give the child the optimal amount of help yet leave him or her as independent as possible. In order to help without completely taking over, adults can use a system of physical, visual, and verbal prompts; they can also organize the environment in ways that encourage practice. Other suggestions about how to practice are provided in the following chapters.

# Facilitating Effective Practice

**P**hysical skills can be practiced in various ways. Some parents and teachers show children exactly what to do and have them do drills in which they repeat a task again and again in order to memorize it. Others draw children out through questioning; they give a child a problem to solve or a goal to reach and ask the child to find his or her own solution. Different approaches to practice can bring about different responses from children, and some approaches work better than others, depending on what the teacher wants to achieve. Some approaches are more likely to have a positive emotional or psychological effect on learners, whereas other approaches may result in quick gains in skill performance but less long-term learning. This chapter provides suggestions about creating practice opportunities that effectively teach skills.

## STRUCTURING PRACTICE

The key to learning a skill is to engage in *appropriate* practice, which may not always mean *perfect* practice. That is, practicing the very same thing over and over—and doing so without error—may not lead to the best learning and retention of a skill. It is certainly true, however, that learning a skill demands practice and that, for the most part, more practice is better. Highly skilled athletes practice their key skills thousands (if not millions) of times, and many, or perhaps most, of these practice trials are done alone, without a teacher or coach.

Practicing simple skills early in life can equip a child to participate in more difficult skill performances later. When children learn skills, the knowledge they gain is broader than just the physical know-how for doing a particular skill. They also gain knowledge *about* the skill and about how to use it. For example, if Terry learns how to jump from a low step at age 3, he does more than learn to bend his knees, swing his arms, and apply force to the stair as he launches himself from it. He also learns that a high step is harder to jump from, that it might be easier to jump into water than onto cement, that it takes a certain amount of time to jump and thus he should wait until the path is clear, and that he can jump from either of the bottom two stairs but not from the third stair up.

In fact, poor physical skill in later childhood has been attributed by several researchers to a skill-learning gap (Wall, 2004) or a practice deficit (Bouffard et al., 1996) that prevents a child from acquiring the knowledge needed for participating in more demanding environments as he or she gets older. This does not mean that certain skills are necessarily prerequisites of others (a view that has been held by experts in physical activity for many years), but rather that children learn different kinds of knowledge as they learn and practice new skills, and the knowledge they gain can be applied to other situations or activities. At age 4 or 5, a child can practice jumping off of platforms or boxes of varying heights and can do so at his or her own pace; she learns how to bend her knees, how to land softly, and how to time each of the movements in her arms and legs. This knowledge can then be applied, at age 6 or 7, during a fast-paced game of tag as she leaps to avoid a tag. In other words, practice provides children with a way to learn *about* a skill as well as how to do it, and both kinds of knowledge are important to the child's ability to use the skill in various circumstances throughout life.

According to practice experts, learning during practice is most effective when the goal or task is clear in the mind of the learner, when it is neither too hard nor too easy, when the practice environment is supportive, and when the learner has opportunities to make and correct mistakes. In shooting a basketball, for example, the learner should know whether the practice goal is to get a high arc on the shot or simply to have the ball hit the target. Similarly, in hanging from a horizontal bar, having a vague idea of hanging upside down does not lead to the same speed of learning as knowing that one must bend the knees and tuck the feet through and over the bar between the hands; thus the practice goal might be for the learner to bring the legs up between the hands rather than the outside of them. Teachers can allow students to choose the skills they want to learn, yet still give them information about key skill features so that they can hold useful learning goals in mind while they practice. In fact, knowing the key features of the skill will make you a better teacher even as it makes your child a better learner.

Practice bears more fruit when entered into enthusiastically, willingly, and with motivation to get better rather than just put in the time. For that reason, practice episodes may be more beneficial if they are kept fairly short, done when the learner has shown a desire to achieve in a particular skill, and conducted in a context that is supportive and enjoyable so that the learner is eager to repeat the experience. Learning is an active process in which the learner's progress is strongly influenced not only by physical effort but also by the cognitive effort that he or she brings to bear during practice.

" **Freema, age 7: I used to be able not to do cartwheels very good, but now I can. I practiced A LOT!** "

Researchers have made progress toward understanding what happens cognitively during practice. Learning physical skills, like learning math or reading, is dependent on thinking. Thus researchers want to understand what occurs when a learner is taught a new skill under a certain regimen of practice. These researchers have examined ways in which the type of practice, as well as its scheduling or timing, may increase the learning and remembering of a skill. For example, they have shown that thinking about a skill between practice trials enhances the effectiveness of those trials. They have shown that the frequency and timing of practice trials, and the type and amount of feedback, all have an impact on how much is learned and what is learned.

# ENCOURAGING SELF-REGULATED PRACTICE

Practice can be self-regulated, and, in fact, learners often do practice on their own. Children often repeat a new skill with a good deal of satisfaction without being asked or told to do so. When Rachel, for example, was first learning to do the cartwheel, her eyes continually searched for space in which to try it out. As a result, she performed hundreds of practice trials on her own, and the skill became almost automatic. In fact, during this learning period, when she was about 8 years old, conversations with her were peppered with her performances of cartwheels as long as there was sufficient empty space at her feet. One moment she would be talking, and in the next instant she would be doing a cartwheel right on the spot! In another example, when Terry was learning to catch with a glove, he used every means possible to adapt his tossing of the ball to himself. He practiced throwing the ball higher to give himself sufficient time to get under it with his glove, and later he began to shorten the height of the throws to make himself move faster, thus making the task harder. His production of self-created trials led him to become a confident and skilled catcher (and tosser).

Adults find that when play equipment is left in sight and is available, children of all ages tend to pick it up and practice a particular skill on their own. Thus parents can encourage self-regulated practice by, for example, leaving a ball and glove in plain sight, setting up a playground apparatus in the backyard, or clearing a large open space in the basement. The practice is self-regulated because the learner answers such questions as what to do, how many times to do it, and when and where to do it. Once a learner has a general idea of the task demands, he or she may keep doing the task again and again in an effort to improve performance. Usually this kind of practice is highly motivated and very fruitful, provided that the learner can apply strategies to detect errors and make corrections. In these cases, it may be best if a parent or instructor lets such activity continue uninterrupted!

For some children, however, self-regulated practice may be difficult if the key features of the skill are not readily apparent. For example, solo practice may be frustrating for a child who does not know that it is important to line up the face (strings) of a tennis racket with the target (e.g., a wall) and to hit the ball lightly enough that the return bounce comes at a manageable speed. Self-directed practice may be very difficult for children who are wanting to learn how to get into the right position to hang from their knees on the climber. The fact that children *can* practice on their own doesn't necessarily mean that they will do so, or that they will practice in a way that enables them to become skillful. A mixture of self-regulated practice and instructor-guided practice is optimal for learning new skills and increasing playground skill repertoires.

# INSTRUCTOR-GUIDED PRACTICE

Playground skills are no different from other life skills. Would we expect a child to play the violin simply by watching and listening? Yet the kind of instructional effort expended on teaching children music, reading, math, and gymnastics is rarely invested in helping them learn physical skills for free play on the playground. However, it is important that children develop playground skills, and practice and instruction can help a child learn them. Some children will simply *not* acquire playground skills without instructional help. For these children, acquiring skill for the playground goes a long way toward ensuring that they have the opportunity to engage with peers, learn social skills, and be included in games and activities. Besides, being able to do physical skills on the playground is fun, and being competent helps children feel good about themselves. Most children love physical practice, too—or they can, if it is well planned.

# PRACTICING DIFFERENT VERSIONS OF THE SAME SKILL

People often practice the same skill over and over in the same way; teachers and coaches encourage their students or players to do, say, 20 consecutive turns in exactly the same way. Research suggests, however, that this may not make for good practice. Many researchers in the field of skill acquisition believe firmly that variability of practice is a positive thing when learning a new skill. Rather than do a task repeatedly in exactly the same way, it is better to vary it in some dimension. After all, how often does one encounter a situation that requires performance of identical movements over and over?

Let's consider an example. In helping a child practice catching a ball that rebounds from a wall, a parent or teacher may toss the ball against the wall. The child's job is to catch the ball, either as it rebounds directly from the wall or after it bounces off the ground. Tradition would suggest throwing the ball against the wall in the very same way (i.e., with the same speed, height, angle, and place of rebound) for many trials until the child gets good at catching the expected rebound. The idea of this kind of practice is that the ball's flight gets to be highly predictable and the child becomes better able to catch it.

The principle of variability in practice, however, suggests that the ball should be tossed against the wall at different heights, different speeds, and different angles and that it should rebound to different places. In fact, the toss should be done a little differently each time. In this way, the child has to problem-solve each time he or she tries to catch the ball. By making a new "plan" each time, the catcher may be establishing rules or guidelines (whether conscious or unconscious) about the flights of balls and how to intercept them. Researchers think that expert ballplayers develop both implicit and explicit rules about ball flights based on all of their experiences with ball flights, and that they use these rules to interpret the information they get from seeing the very first images of, say, a ball coming off a baseball bat. They catch sight of the ball going toward the bat and the contact point, and they then make predictions about how far the ball will travel, how high, how fast. This phenomenon may explain why outstanding goalies can react to a puck coming off a hockey stick or a soccer ball coming off a foot before other people even know what is happening. They have had thousands of different kinds of practice trials, and they have developed rules of thumb that tell them where the puck will go based on their very first glimpse of it. Even when they have never seen a puck approach the goal in a certain way, they can predict where it will go and when it will arrive because they use rules based on previous experience to make predictions in new situations.

Practicing the same skill differently, then, can be beneficial, even if it seems to be harder at first. Thus if you are helping a child learn to catch a rebounding ball, it might make sense to mix soft tosses—both high and low—with harder (faster) high and low balls. You might toss the ball so that it rebounds to the child's left and then to the right, or high and then low, or soft and then hard. In this way, the child will have an opportunity to learn what flight patterns are like and to establish rules in his or her mind that may

> **Jerome, age 8:** Like before, I couldn't do the rings, so I kept on doing it every summer, kept on trying, kept on trying, and now I can do them.

help with future catches! The child will gain knowledge about ball flights, rebound angle, and speed that will help him or her deal with new rebounds when they are encountered. It is not hard to imagine how important thinking is to this activity!

Take care, however, not to make each trial so hard that the child always fails. Help the child do something different each time but strive to make each of the turns manageable. You can make initial attempts at a skill easier by giving cues—for example, "Here comes a faster one" or "I might throw this one high or I might throw it low. Be ready!" If the child experiences some success on moderately hard tasks, along with success on easy tasks and some failures on harder tasks, then he or she can develop confidence and competence in adapting to varied situations. It is crucial to make sure that the child knows you think failing at some of the tasks is a good way to learn. That is, errorless performance may *not* be the best way to learn, and it certainly won't help a child know what he or she can and cannot do!

# PRACTICING DIFFERENT SKILLS TOGETHER

A second firm principle—which differs from traditional approaches to movement skill learning but is well supported by research—holds that different skills are learned better if practiced together rather than in isolation. Furthermore, skills should be practiced in an unpredictable order. This principle resembles the notion of the variability of practice but goes a step further by saying that it is better to practice catching a tossed ball, kicking a ball, and catching a bouncing ball in a mixed-up order than it is to do 30 turns in a row of catching a tossed ball, then 30 trials of kicking a ball, and then 30 trials of catching a bouncing ball. Because this idea goes against what we have traditionally experienced in physical education or sport instruction, it can be hard to accept, but it is supported by plenty of research. In order to get the maximum benefit from practice time, we should practice skills in an unpredictable order and under different circumstances each time. Who would have guessed?

The theory behind this approach holds that when the task changes every time, the person doing the skill has to put a lot of cognitive effort (thinking) into each practice trial. This increased attention enables the learner to establish better and more useful rules to guide his or her movement behavior. Put another way, the child solves a movement problem each time the skill changes, and it is this action of solving a problem—not just doing what he or she did a moment ago—that constitutes learning. In contrast, when practice means doing the same task again and again and again in a "drill" format, the learner faces *decreasing* need to think about the response, plan it, and sequence it. In that case, the child doesn't have to pay a lot of attention to tracking the ball with his or her eyes or anticipating where it will go, because he or she already knows from the last turn. Thus, little cognitive energy is put into determining the movement solution for each turn. In such circumstances, the child doesn't have to concentrate much and doesn't learn much. The learner can get by with paying very little attention to what is being done, and the movement response becomes automatic, whereas in the real play world naturally varying situations require children to adapt their responses.

This effect has been well demonstrated for all kinds of learners, including novices and experts and children with intellectual disability. At first, children may struggle a bit with this approach, but in the long run they learn skills better, remember them longer, and transfer them to other conditions more effectively. With very difficult or complex skills some initial "blocked" practice (repetitions of the same skill) may be beneficial to make sure the child actually understands what the skill entails (what are its goal and key features).

To put this approach into practice when, for example, taking your child into the backyard to play catch, you would play in such a way that the child doesn't know whether the ball will be bounced, thrown in the air, or rolled on any given turn. You would also vary the speed, path, and timing of the delivery each time. You can ensure that the child has some early success by giving alerts (e.g., "Here it comes with a bounce to the left side") so that the ball's path is more predictable, but very soon you should begin changing the characteristics of the task each time you deliver the ball. Of course, it is important to keep the tasks within the child's range of ability; the child must have some opportunities for success in order to remain motivated to practice. Thus each task should be both challenging *and* attainable. Finding this balance can be difficult, but it can be done by keeping an eye on the child's success rate. A perceptive and sensitive instructor can detect when it is time to alter conditions, thus demanding less or more, in order to provide challenge *and* enable success for the child learner.

# CONCLUSION

Some of the traditional practice styles that many of us have experienced in sport and physical education may place unnecessary limits on skill learning. Intuitively, many of us have tried to use repetition of the very same skill again and again as a good method for learning and even for practicing on our own. And some children have learned effectively in this manner. But the research now seems to say that it is better to practice different skills in sequence or to practice the same skill in different ways. While this approach may not yield as much early success for a particular skill, it results in better learning and better retention of skills in the long run.

Self-determined practice may be the very best practice there is, because it means that children are motivated to learn. It is also noteworthy that a child, left to make his or her own decisions, usually begins to alter a skill in order to increase the challenge and maintain interest in much the same way that researchers recommend!

# Teaching in a Positive Climate

**M**ohammed attends a learn-to-swim program for the first time at the age of four. He is afraid of water, but soon finds himself comfortable enough to sit on the edge of the pool with his mother and dangle his feet in the water. We may not know exactly why he feels comfortable (is it the teacher's smile? the instructions she is giving? the way the poolside is organized, with toys both in and out of the water?), but we can be pretty sure that the behavior of the teacher in the pool is a major source of information for him. Given another teacher and another pool, Mohammed might not let go of his mother's hand and may refuse to put any part of his body in the water. His behavioral outcomes are strongly influenced by what he perceives (and *not* what he is told!) about the instructional context.

When learners enter and spend time in an instructional environment (or context), their behavioral outcomes will be determined by the interaction of the goals of the tasks that are to be done there, their own perceptions of the environment in which these tasks are to be accomplished, and their perceptions of their own capacities to accomplish those tasks (Davis & van Emmerik, 1995). In settings where these tasks include public physical performances, the perceived match of one's capacity to the demands of that environment might be particularly important to the behavioral outcomes (what one does).

This chapter addresses the overall learning context—the tone or climate of the instructional setting—as well as ways in which it can be optimized. The climate of instruction involves the way in which the child interprets the teacher's goals for a given instructional episode. It doesn't matter whether the teacher is a parent, coach, or recreation instructor. Teachers do things in a certain way, and children interpret what a teacher does and says in order to understand what that teacher wants. That is, a child detects what a teacher values and what the teacher is trying to achieve in the instructional setting. Whether or not a child's perceptions of the teacher's intentions are entirely accurate, they do guide his or her behavior and emotions. The *perceived climate*, then, involves how the child sees the instructional episode and what the child interprets the teacher's behaviors to mean. There are two main types of perceived climate: performance and mastery.

## PERFORMANCE CLIMATES

In an instructional setting, a *performance climate* is one where the best performance is highly valued, especially if it is deemed better than the performances of others who are also trying to do the skill. In other words, the teacher communicates that the goal of the instructional episode is to achieve superior performance as compared with the performance of other participants. In this climate, winning and being the best are perceived by the child to be most important. Teachers reward the best performance, make a big fuss over who was the winner or the best, and make social comparisons between learners: "And the *winners* are the red team!" "Nancy is the best in the class!"

A child may perceive a situation as a performance climate based on certain teacher behaviors. One key behavior is a teacher's inclination to say things to a person in a way that everyone can hear; that is, the teacher gives feedback to learners in a public way. For instance, the instructor might say, "Do this the way Stefan does it. He's really good at it." In addition, the teacher may design activities in a way that promotes competition between people and give rewards—not just praise and attention but physical rewards (e.g., medals, ribbons, choice of equipment, a chance to demonstrate)—for being the best. Many fitness testing programs, for instance, have award structures (e.g., gold, silver, and bronze ribbons for high-level performers and mere participation awards for others) that may lead a child to perceive a performance climate. Such practices say very clearly to a child that the teacher places a higher value on being excellent (i.e., better than others) in this activity than on, say, being better than he or she was before.

Parents establish this kind of learning climate when they put pressure on their children to be "better"—often, better than someone else. They may criticize mistakes, make fun of errors, or say (implicitly or explicitly), "That isn't good enough." They may even yell at their children in a public setting or ask them, "Why didn't you pass the ball when you saw Todd in the clear?" Despite television commercials that satirize this kind of communication between parents and children, it still happens everywhere.

In a performance climate, teachers or instructors exert complete control of what is to be done; they decide what skills will be practiced and what activities will be performed. They decide what is valued, and these tasks are the focus of instruction. Children who find themselves in this kind of instructional climate may feel that they do not get to choose what to do. They simply have to do what the teacher wants them to do. The teacher makes all the decisions.

A performance climate that emphasizes winning or comparisons between children may be a comfortable one for children who are highly skilled, are the best in their group, and like demonstrating their skill. They are likely to win, to receive a reward, and generally to get positive attention from the instructor or parent. As long as they are winning, they may work hard to demonstrate their competence. These kids love to go to practices where goals are counted, drills are competitive, and it is clearly acknowledged how skilled they are. They feel good because they think they are the best, or at least among the best. On the playground, they may even set up situations where winners and losers are named, because the results are likely to favor them. They like competition.

This type of climate is much less encouraging, however, for children who lack skill or do not perform well in public settings. Children who already think they are not very good will not want to take part in climates that are based on performance. They may be uncomfortable in such climates, and they may be sensitive to the fact that high and low achievement are valued differently; they may also realize that teachers have lower expectations of poor performers. They may prefer to avoid being in such situations if they can, and it may seem pointless to them even to try. If parents persist in using this kind of approach, their child may develop very negative emotions and eventually resist situations in which the parent is the coach or teacher.

Thus a performance climate can be punishing for children who are not very good and for those who really want to be the best but cannot do so. If they are no longer able to demonstrate that they are among the best, they may begin to withdraw from the activity or try to devalue it. Such a child might say, "Well, if I can't be the best, then I won't try. And anyway this is a stupid game." Or the child might simply think, *This is no fun if I can't win!*

Since the instructor's tight control of the performance climate allows little room for decision making by children, a child participating in such a climate can only perform those skills that the instructor calls for and hope (or wish) to do them well. Children who feel they cannot do well at the selected skills may want to avoid exposing their inadequacy and thus may seek to withdraw in any way they can. They may try to minimize the importance of the activity by publicly claiming that the game is boring or unfair. Children in this position have been observed to fake injury or illness, to repeatedly tie their shoes, to make frequent trips to the bathroom or water fountain, to distract others from the activity, and generally to avoid taking their turns. (Many of us have experienced situations in which a child ducks to the back of the line again before actually taking his turn!) When you see this kind of behavior in a child, you may at first think that the child is just behaving badly. The truth, however, may be that the child is responding to feelings of discomfort with the instructional climate. Kids have to protect themselves and their feelings, and in a threatening situation like this (threatening because the child fears looking stupid or feeling incompetent) it only makes sense for them to find ways to avoid a negative outcome or to minimize the importance of the activities in order to save face.

Instructors may think that as long as they are treating all children in the same way—saying the same things and giving consistent instructions—children will benefit equally. But it has been shown that even when the same instructions and feedback are given to all children, cues may be interpreted differently by children according to their own dispositions and perceptions of themselves. In a performance climate, for instance, if a teacher says, "Good, Robert! You hit the target!" the comment could be interpreted by Robert to mean that he is

> **"Chloe, age 8: They have pylons and they sort of race to see who can dribble the puck around them. . . . I'm not very good and I'm not very good at handling pucks . . . so when I'm last my friends might make fun of me. They have stopwatches . . . and whoever gets there first they tell their time and then the last one sort of gets . . . it just feels unfair when you hardly know how to do it. . . . I feel sort of embarrassed . . . unhappy . . . just really bad."**

skillful and his performance is valued by the instructor, and this is the likely interpretation if he has been one of the best in his group. However, if Robert does not perceive himself to be one of the best, he may interpret the comment as a statement about his previous lack of success. He may think, *She's just saying that to make me feel good. She knows I only hit the target once in a million tries!* Thus he may find the statement about this one successful try to be almost humiliating: as a result, he may feel demotivated. These perceptions become a very real and relevant part of the context, and it is not difficult to see that different interpretations can lead to quite different behaviors!

# MASTERY CLIMATES

*Mastery climates* are ones in which the instructor communicates that he or she values effort and practice and getting better at a skill—that trying and getting better are far more important than being better than someone else. Feedback is given respectfully and privately and is not based on social comparison (rather than "You didn't kick the ball as hard as Harry," a parent or teacher might say, "Go ahead and try to kick the ball *hard*!" or simply, "Wow, that was a hard kick! You really stepped into it!"). In addition, instructors using this model provide different feedback and instructions to different children according to their needs. This type of learning situation emphasizes the learning process, and rewards are not given for being the best as compared with others but for making progress—or at least trying to do so.

Thus a mastery instructional climate is more likely to encourage children to engage in positive learning behaviors such as practicing, trying to improve, and paying attention to the task. This type of climate encourages strategies that help children learn and improve rather than strategies that lead to winning (we all know where these strategies can lead us—to actions such as cheating, pushing, tripping, and interfering, and sometimes to competing against someone you are already sure you can beat!).

This philosophy does not mean that the instructor should give excessive positive reinforcement. Children get wise to this. They may well know that they are not doing well or are not getting better, and in this case the instructor's exuberance may not be interpreted in the way it is intended. In fact, the child may think, *He's just saying "Good try" because he knows I will never be able to do this.* Providing positive feedback from time to time may help to keep students motivated as they learn, and in a mastery climate this feedback focuses as much on the effort put into learning as it does on the actual level of performance or the outcome of the skills being learned. It puts emphasis on searching for a strategy rather than on choosing the best strategy.

One of the hallmarks of a mastery climate is that the instructor gives choices to learners in order to increase their motivation. In other words, the instructor gives the learner high autonomy, or a good measure of personal control over what is to be done and learned. Being able to choose what he or she does generally increases a child's motivation to do it, repeat it, and try hard at it. In contrast, motivation to work hard *decreases* when people feel that they are being told what to do and kept under surveillance while they do it. In a performance climate, the teacher decides what is to be practiced and learned; in a mastery climate, there is room for the child to decide what and how to practice.

There is evidence that mastery motivational climates lead to improvement in children's perceptions of their own competence and in time spent on task. Since there is little or no public comparison of one child with another child, each child is free to work at his or her own pace and to risk trying and failing. It doesn't seem as bad to fail or miss if no one seems to be noticing, or if the child is trying hard to learn the skill because it is something that he or she has chosen. Of course, children will still see (and possibly compare their performances with) the performances of others, but they feel sure that the teacher isn't very interested in such comparisons, and that in itself can make all the difference. Thus a mastery climate allows children to use their personal information to reward and motivate themselves ("I'm not as good as Barry, but I am better than I was yesterday!") rather than rely on a teacher's or parent's judgment.

The many skills involved in each activity included in this book allow you to provide children with meaningful choices that help establish a mastery climate. Children can choose what they want to learn. They can assess their likelihood of success and failure at each task and choose the ones that will keep them most positively motivated. On the swing, for instance, there are both easy and hard tasks that will allow a child to participate in swinging activity. You can show the child illustrations of all the choices for the swing and let the child decide which skills he or she feels ready to learn.

You can also try to communicate genuine appreciation for each of these tasks regardless of their level of difficulty. That is, rather than pushing the child to try the most difficult skills or suggesting that the hard tasks are more important than the easier ones, you can make sure that the child knows you think the skills are *all* important! Maybe, for example, your child wants to sit down and pump the swing rather than stand up and pump. Both skills are good ones for playing on the swing, and either can be used on the playground to be active and involved. So make it clear that they are both very valuable skills and let the child choose; remember, it is likely that the child's motivation to learn a skill will be greater if he or she chooses it than if he or she is told to learn it. You can still give guidance about which skills might be harder or easier, but let the child make the final choice. If all of the choices are portrayed as acceptable, the child will feel more autonomy and may interpret the climate of the instruction to be one of mastery rather than one of performance.

In a mastery climate, then, children who are not taking part in certain popular activities (e.g., playing catch, using the zip line) are shown the many options available for engaging in that activity and are encouraged to choose something to learn to do. They can be helped in one-on-one instructional episodes that are short and positive or in the midst of group activity or instruction where the climate encourages mastery of the skill. In this climate, children are not compared with others. When they are given advice about how to do a skill better, the advice is given privately and positively. Rewards and awards are generally not used; if they are employed, they are used to recognize effort and progress, not absolute performance.

Table 8.1 summarizes the differences between mastery and performance climates.

### Table 8.1    Comparison of Performance and Mastery Climates

|  | Performance climate | Mastery climate |
|---|---|---|
| Emphasis | Winning | Trying |
|  | Being the best | Practicing |
| Feedback | Public | Private |
|  | Rewards | Depends on child |
| Instruction | Teacher decides what is to be learned | Teacher gives choices |
|  | Certain tasks valued | All tasks valued |
|  | Comparisons made between children | Self-self comparisons |
| Self-perceptions | Low autonomy | High autonomy |
|  | Poor perceptions of competence except for the highest skilled | Fosters positive perceptions of self |

# COMPETITIVE AND COOPERATIVE ACTIVITIES

Competitive activities often tend to lead to performance climates because many of the characteristics of competition are shared with performance climates. That is, there is usually a winner or a winning team, people try to perform better than others, and much emphasis (and value) may be placed on being the best. As a result, children with strong self-perceptions may do well in most competitive contexts. They may even be able to withstand losing in these situations by attributing the losses to other people or factors. As Jerome (age 8) says about competitive contexts, "Someone wants to beat you. Someone wants to be better than you, some just are gooder at it and they feel so strong about themselves, that when they lose they say, 'That wasn't me. That was someone else. That wasn't my fault.'"

However, competitive activities don't necessarily need to be performance climates; they *can* be fun for everyone. That is, instructors can create contexts for competitive activities that place importance on learning to play, playing by the rules, trying one's best, and being part of the team. At the same time, they can downplay the importance of the score and of who wins. Positive and genuine support for effort, and for simply participating in any legitimate role, can go a long way toward helping children feel comfortable when engaging in competitive activities.

Cooperative activities similarly can be experienced in both mastery and performance climates. In a mastery climate, cooperative activities emphasize the degree of collaboration being demonstrated and the value of each contribution regardless of its influence on the outcome. In a performance climate, cooperative activities may be valued more for the outcome itself, so that each child involved feels a significant responsibility to make a *capable* contribution to the effort (Ames, 1992). In this situation a child who cannot make the same contribution to the effort as another child can may feel inadequate. So cooperative activities, once considered the answer to involving children with a wide range of skills in the same activity setting, should be considered carefully so that no one child is put at risk.

Despite a teacher's attempts to develop a mastery climate, competitive and cooperative activities may lead to comparisons between children, suggesting that both competitive and cooperative physical activities can be offered in performance and mastery climates. The critical thing for instructors to consider is each child's perception of the climate in which instruction or participation is taking place. All children will not see the climate the same way, and instructors will have a special responsibility to make sure that vulnerable children are not put at risk of having negative emotions in the activity setting.

# CONCLUSION

Participation and instruction take place in contexts that are interpreted by children to support different outcomes. In performance climates, children perceive instructors to place value on winning, being better than another, and performance outcomes (how far, how fast, how many points). In mastery climates, children perceive that the instructor places value on trying, learning, and having fun. Instructors of playground skills are encouraged to maintain a mastery climate by avoiding comparing children with each other; by providing children with choices about what, when, and where to learn; and by giving private encouragement and feedback. Instructors can also reinforce positive learning behaviors, such as trying a skill, trying hard, trying again, paying attention, making decisions about how to accomplish a task, and making small improvements in performance. Mastery climates have been shown to be the most productive learning environments for children.

# Playing Games

Sharon Baker
Jane Watkinson

**P**lay is normally considered to have no clear goal, no beginning or ending, and no winners or losers. It is just kids sharing space and cooperating in activities that are joyful. Games, on the other hand, are often thought of as being competitive, having clear goals, and producing winners and losers. Some of the simple games we see younger children playing serve as stepping stones or scaffolds between play and games—and between isolated activity and cooperative interaction. In this latter role, they provide a mechanism for introducing children who otherwise would not have met. During the first year of school, these apparently simple games serve an important transitional role. They facilitate the change from social interaction at home and in preschool settings to social interaction in the more complex outdoor playground that is typical of the primary school context. These simpler games also provide an introduction to the increasingly complex rules that govern the more formal games of the playground.

In preschool, interaction is often moderated by a teacher or leader who brings children together, supervises play, and interrupts activity or behavior that can be problematic. On the primary school playground, however, supervisors are typically much less engaged and much less intrusive. This is the place where children have to independently play together, learn rules, and eventually engage in the games that are part of the local culture.

## TAG: A UNIVERSAL GAME

While playground games differ by gender, by age, and even from school to school, one particular type of game—tag—and its modifications (including chase) have been observed in virtually every study of playground activity on both sides of the Atlantic Ocean. Tag is among the most popular of the simple games found on the playground and has been played by nearly every child—boy or girl, young or old (Blatchford, Baines, & Pellegrini, 2003).

More important, being able to play tag effectively is a true asset for a child. It provides a vehicle for interaction with others at its most simple level. Who would have thought that so much could be learned through tag? The game is full of techniques and strategies used in complex and sophisticated sports more likely to be seen in later childhood years. Thus, if children become skillful in the game of tag, they may be better prepared to participate in more complex games such as soccer. Here is a list of the basic skills required in the game of tag, many of which are needed for success in various competitive sports.

- *Knowing how and when to adopt a multidirectional ready position*: This position, with feet about shoulder-width apart and staggered, knees comfortably bent, and weight on the balls of the feet, allows for quick movement in any direction. (Other ready positions are better for unidirectional movement, as in sprinting.)

- *Keeping weight over the body's base of support*: This skill involves keeping the body well balanced over its base (usually the feet) so that one can quickly change directions without falling over or losing control.

- *Learning to change direction and speed of movement*: Children learn to speed up quickly, stop without warning, and change direction without giving away their next move.

- *Developing an awareness of space*: Children learn to constantly scan the play area, see empty spaces they can move into, analyze who is where at a given moment, and anticipate where another child will be in an instant (Belka, 1998).

- *Dodging*: This skill involves avoiding being tagged by moving various body parts away from the person doing the tagging—for example, by twirling, stretching, or simply changing direction quickly (Belka, 1998).

- *Deceiving and faking:* This skill involves giving a false impression of where one is going or giving no impression of what one is planning to do. Children learn to confuse each other by disguising which way they will be moving, how fast they will be going, or at which instant they will move. They learn, for instance, to use their eyes or head to transmit one message about their intended direction while actually moving in another direction.

These strategies are different for the chaser and for the person being chased. The child who is "It" chases the other children and attempts to tag them. The "Not-It" children run away from It in an effort to avoid being tagged. Thus the chaser must learn the ready position, make quick stops and direction changes, and tag gently, whereas the dodgers (the Not-Its) must make quick stops and direction changes, commit to running in one direction, and learn to fake.

As tag games change between the ages of 3 and 8, they involve increasing physical skill, more difficult techniques, and more complex strategic content; in addition, rules become more important. The first tag-like game is simple chasing, which requires physical skill (running with significant speed) and understanding of a simple relational rule: "I run and you follow!" This activity develops into a more complex one: "I run and you try to catch me by touching or tagging me!" Children can generally understand this activity at 3 years of age. By the time they are 8 years old, both the essential physical skills (acceleration, changes of direction, dodging) and the rules and strategies (e.g., "You can tag me only when your eyes are closed" or "You cannot retag your tagger") have become more difficult and complex.

Can you prepare a child or children for these changes in rules and strategy even as you help them enhance their physical skills? Of course you can! And you can start by understanding the basic forms that tag can take.

Tag has many variations, but they seem to fit into four basic categories: traditional, manipulative, equipment, and line. Traditional tag includes all versions in which one person is designated as It and multiple other participants are designated as Not-It. The person who is It must chase and tag the Not-It children. When someone is successfully tagged, one of two outcomes occurs: Either the tagged child becomes It (this is basic tag) or he or she must do something to get free again. You might remember, for instance, a game called freeze tag, in which a Not-It person who has not been tagged might do something to free the tagged children, such as touch them, go through their legs or under their arms, or run a circle around them. In this version, the child who is It remains It until the end of the game or until the children decide that it is another child's turn to be It. Traditional tag (where one person is It) is straightforward in that it requires no objects or equipment and can be played anywhere. It is likely to be the most frequent activity on your local playground—and the one that every child needs to know how to take part in.

Manipulative tag is similar to traditional tag except that the person who is It must use a held or projected object to tag the other participants—for instance, a ball (ball tag), snowball (snow tag), or clothespin (clothespin tag). This style of tag can be played in a wide variety of settings, and the type of implement used is almost unlimited. However, in addition to using the skills (e.g., running, dodging, accelerating) required in basic tag, participants in some versions of manipulative tag must also be able to throw for accuracy, often while moving. The target is usually moving too! Thus a less agile or mobile child might be able to successfully tag others without catching up to them.

Equipment tag also comes in a few varieties, but its key feature is that the children play on or around large playground equipment rather than on an open field. Specifically, the game is played on slides, monkey bars, poles, and climbers; as a result, players are forced to use various skills (e.g., hanging, dropping, jumping down, swinging, climbing) in addition to running and dodging. Two variations of equipment tag are grounders and hide-and-seek tag. In grounders, the It person can verbally tag someone by calling out, "Grounders!" as the others move around the equipment; if a child is on the ground when the call is made, then he or she is considered tagged. Games of equipment tag cast a different person as It for each round.

Line tag is quite a different type of game. The person designated as It begins at one end of an area, and all other participants stand in a line facing him or her. After some type of verbal call, the children attempt to get from one location (the starting line) to another without being tagged; boundaries are usually established to indicate the area in which the children may run. Any child who is tagged becomes It *along with* the first It. Thus the game accelerates as it progresses and a team of Its is accumulated. Variations, some of which are described later in more detail, include Mr. Wolf and British bulldog. Line tag works best when played in an open, unobstructed area with clearly marked boundaries.

The following activities describe eight types of tag—two from each of the four basic categories. In the interest of consistency, the name *Tommy* is used to portray what the It child does, while *Jada* indicates the role of a Not-It child. Each description provides the main goal of the game, the basic rules for both Tommy and Jada, and a short explanation of the strategies that each child might use to improve his or her performance. These descriptions are given so that you can help all children know the simple rules that differentiate one version from another. Game strategies are also important, and though they are often implicit (i.e., children may not be able to express them) they are essential elements for successful inclusion in the games.

## BASIC TAG

This type of traditional tag can be played by any number of children of a variety of ages in any number of locations—on the playground, in a house, or even in a swimming pool.

### Main Goal

Tommy tries to tag Jada; if tagged, Jada becomes the new It.

### Rules

1. Children must remain within designated boundaries.
2. Tommy must tag other children with his hand (unless agreed upon otherwise).
3. Runners must understand that when they are tagged they become It and that when they tag someone else they are no longer It.
4. Many children use the "no tag back" rule, which means that once Tommy tags Jada, she may not immediately tag Tommy again; she must tag another child instead.

### Strategies

For Tommy (It):

- Make a plan for catching someone (Jada).
- Start slowly and wait for Jada to make the first move.
- Pretend to chase Jada, then go after another runner.
- Trap Jada and decrease her potential escape routes.

For Jada (Not-It):

- Quickly change directions or fake one way and then move another.
- Always leave herself two or more escape routes to ensure that she does not get stuck in a position with no way out.
- Maintain the ready position but do not run until chased; otherwise, she may run right into Tommy.
- Hide, or slow Tommy down by putting something or someone between herself and Tommy.

## SKUNK TAG

This type of tag also falls within the traditional category. It can be helpful when you want to incorporate different skills into children's repertoires (e.g., the skill of balancing on one foot), and the waiting skill can be varied in order to change the skills that children practice during the game (e.g., jumping jacks for coordination, hopping for balance).

### Main Goal

It (i.e., Tommy, acting as a skunk who has an imaginary stink bomb) tries to tag as many people as possible. Jada tries to avoid being tagged by Tommy;

if she is tagged, she must pretend she has just been sprayed by a skunk and should stand with one leg up and one arm under the leg to cover her nose.

## Rules

1. One or more skunks must be designated to serve in the role of It.
2. Tommy (It, or the skunk) chases the other players (within designated boundaries) and tries to tag them with the stink bomb.
3. When Jada is tagged, she must stand in the spray position and count to 5 before running free again.
4. Tommy remains It until the children (or supervisors) decide that it is time for a new person to serve as It.

## Strategies

For Tommy (It):

- Start slowly and wait for Jada to make the first move.
- Pretend to chase Jada, then go after another runner.
- Trap Jada and decrease her number of escape routes.

For Jada (Not-It):

- Maintain the ready position but do not run until chased; otherwise, she may run right into Tommy.
- Quickly change directions or fake one way and then move another.
- Always leave herself two or more escape routes to ensure that she does not get stuck in a position with no way out.
- Hide, or slow Tommy down by putting something or someone between herself and Tommy.

## SNOW TAG

This game is a manipulative style of tag. It is, of course, played only at times when snow is available to be packed into a ball. The teacher or supervisor must review safety with the children before the game begins in order to ensure that snow is not thrown at the face or thrown hard enough to injure someone. The target area may be restricted to parts of the body below the waist.

## Main Goal

Tommy tries to tag others by hitting them with a thrown snowball in the designated target area (not the face); Jada tries to avoid being tagged by snowballs.

## Rules

1. Tommy must pick up snow and pack it into balls to throw at the runners.
2. If Tommy successfully hits Jada, then she becomes It.
3. While running, Jada must remain within designated boundaries, and she is not allowed to throw snow when she is not It.

### Strategies

For Tommy (It):

- Always have a snowball in hand ready to be thrown.
- Have several snowballs ready at one time so that if he misses he does not need to pause to make new ones and possibly lose a good target; at least one snowball should remain in his dominant hand at all times.
- Chase Jada until he is in a good position to make a throw at her.
- Fake one way, then quickly change directions to chase someone else; or look at one person but throw at another.
- Pretend to throw (i.e., fake it), then actually throw after Jada reacts (ducks).

### For Jada (Not-It):

- Always leave herself two or more escape routes.
- Do not run in a straight line; rather, change directions quickly and dodge any snowballs that come her way.
- Put something or someone between herself and Tommy.
- Move to a better location (if possible, when Tommy is out of snowballs and has to take time to make more).
- React to thrown snowballs, not to Tommy's throwing motion, in case he fakes a throw.

## BALL TAG

Ball tag is also a manipulative game, but it is very similar to traditional tag. It can be played on equipment or in an open area.

### Main Goal

Tommy tries to tag other players by touching them with a ball that he is holding—not by throwing it. The other children try to avoid being tagged.

### Rules

1. Tommy holds onto the ball at all times and tags with the ball, not with his hand.
2. Tommy may not throw the ball at players.
3. Once Tommy tags Jada, he gives the ball to her and she becomes It.
4. All players must remain within designated boundaries.

### Strategies

For Tommy (It):

- Hold the ball in his dominant hand to make tagging easier.
- Fake one way, then quickly change directions to chase someone else.
- Trap Jada and decrease her number of escape routes.

For Jada (Not-It):

⊙ Maintain the ready position but do not run until being chased.

⊙ Quickly change directions or fake directional changes.

⊙ Always leave herself two or more escape routes.

⊙ Put something or someone between herself and Tommy.

# GROUNDERS

Playing grounders requires playground equipment. Participants must be able to climb on equipment and move around on the ground.

## Main Goal

Tommy tries to physically tag other players on or off of the equipment; he can also catch a player by saying, "Grounders!" when the player is on the ground. Jada tries to avoid being physically tagged by Tommy or being caught on the ground when the call of "Grounders!" is made. Jada can be on the ground when Tommy's eyes are closed (when he is counting), but not when he has finished counting and is chasing or calling out "Grounders!"

## Rules

1. Tommy closes his eyes and counts to 10 while standing on the ground; he then opens his eyes and begins his pursuit.

2. While Tommy is counting, the other children find good hiding places on or around the equipment.

3. Tommy may move around on either the ground or the equipment.

4. Tommy may say, "Grounders!" only when he is physically touching the ground—he may not say it while he is on a piece of equipment.

5. Jada may move around on the equipment or on the ground; however, she runs the risk of being caught in both areas. While on the equipment, she may be physically tagged by Tommy; while on the ground, she may be physically or verbally tagged.

6. Jada may keep her eyes open at all times.

7. After Tommy calls, "Grounders!" he opens his eyes to see if he has caught anyone on the ground. If he has not, he closes his eyes, counts to 10, and begins again. If he *has* caught Jada, then she becomes It and a new round begins.

## Strategies

For Tommy (It):

⊙ Know the equipment very well so that he knows where he is going with his eyes closed.

- Have a quick escape route when mounting a piece of equipment so that he can rapidly hop to the ground and call, "Grounders!" before other players can adjust.
- Pretend to climb onto equipment but jump down quickly when he hears someone on the ground.
- Trap Jada on the equipment and decrease her number of escape routes.
- After a failed, "Grounders!" call, scan the area quickly to see where children are hiding before closing his eyes for the next try.

For Jada (Not-It):

- Remain on equipment as long as possible; do not move off until necessary.
- Run quietly on the ground and know where she is going ahead of time; plan a route.
- Put someone or something between herself and Tommy so that he cannot find her with his eyes closed.
- Always leave herself two or more escape routes.
- Run on the ground only when Tommy is on the equipment, especially when he cannot get down easily.

# HIDE-AND-SEEK TAG

This type of tag works best when played with access to playground equipment; however, it can also be played in an area containing a sufficient number of other objects or buildings to hide behind or in.

## Main Goal

The seeker (Tommy) tries to find and tag runners (e.g., Jada) before they are able to make it back to a designated safe base.

## Rules

1. Tommy closes his eyes and counts to a specified number (e.g., 20, 50, or 100); as he counts, the other children find places to hide within designated boundaries.
2. When Tommy is finished counting, he loudly declares, "Ready or not, here I come."
3. Jada tries to make it back to the safe base without being physically tagged by Tommy.
4. If Jada reaches the base, she is safe for the remainder of the round.
5. The first child to be tagged serves as It in the following round.
6. Tommy needs to tag only one runner before the next round begins.

## Strategies

For Tommy (It):

- Look in a variety of places, since Jada will rarely hide in the same place twice.

- Look and listen carefully for any movement.
- Trap Jada and decrease her number of escape routes.
- Pretend that he does not see Jada hiding and move nonchalantly toward her until he is in a better position to tag her.
- Do not wander too far from home base, even if chasing Jada, because she will eventually have to return there anyway.
- If more than one hider is visible, decide which one he has a better chance of tagging.
- Scan the entire area before zeroing in on specific sections to search.

For Jada (Not-It):

- Hide in a variety of locations, though perhaps occasionally hide in the same place twice in a row if Tommy will not expect it or if it has been a very successful hiding place.
- Plan two pathways back to the home base.
- Always leave herself two or more escape routes.
- Remain very still and quiet, then begin her run back to the base when Tommy is far from her location.

## BRITISH BULLDOG

This game is a type of line tag in which children try to get from one line to the next without getting caught. This game is best played in an open field with two clear lines or boundaries.

### Main Goal

The bulldog (Tommy) tries to tag as many people as possible as they run between the two safe lines. The runners (e.g., Jada) try to be the last one caught by the bulldog (i.e., to make it through as many rounds as possible).

### Rules

1. When all runners are lined up behind the safe line, Tommy calls, "British bulldog!"
2. At this command, the runners sprint from one safe line to the other as Tommy attempts to tag as many as possible.
3. If Tommy fails to catch everyone, which is often the case, the action is repeated with the runners going back to the first line.
4. All players must remain within the designated playing area.
5. Once Jada is caught, she becomes a bulldog *along with* Tommy, and they work together to tag runners.
6. The last person to be caught serves as the first bulldog in the next round.

### Strategies

For Tommy (bulldog):

- Decide before calling, "British bulldog!" who he wants to focus on and chase first.

- When multiple bulldogs occupy the center area, decide on a group strategy regarding who to chase.
- Do not focus on catching many people every time; instead, chase just two or three (or sometimes even one) and aim for those runners that there is a good chance to catch; if the bulldog wants a challenge, aim for faster runners.
- Trap Jada and decrease her number of escape routes.
- Pretend to chase Jada, then go after another runner.

For Jada (runner):

- Maximize her chances by positioning herself behind the start line in such a way that she has, as much as possible, a straight path (free of bulldogs) to the other line.
- If Tommy is clearly focused on her, try to put another player between herself and Tommy.
- Dodge and change directions quickly, while still trying to move toward the other line.

# MR. (OR MRS.) WOLF

This game is also a type of line tag, but it differs from British bulldog in that the runners must get from one safe line *and back* without being tagged by the wolf. It can be played on equipment or in an open area.

### Main Goal

Tommy, serving as Mr. Wolf, needs to call enough numbers (see Rules for more detail) to give himself a chance to tag at least one person when he decides that it is "Lunch time!" The runners (e.g., Jada) try to progress as far as possible while avoiding being tagged by the wolf.

### Rules

1. Tommy stands away from all others and turns his back toward them. He should stand at least a dozen steps away, but not more than 30 steps.
2. The runners all start behind a designated line and ask, "What time is it, Mr. [or Mrs.] Wolf?"
3. Tommy responds by giving a time between 1 and 12 o'clock.
4. The runners take the appropriate number of steps forward (e.g., 3 o'clock means three steps).
5. This pattern continues until Tommy thinks the runners have gone far enough, whereupon he responds to the question with "Lunch time!"
6. At this command, the runners (e.g., Jada) scamper back to the starting line while Tommy turns around and tries to tag at least one of them; if tagged, Jada joins Tommy as a wolf in the next round.
7. If Tommy fails to tag anyone, he remains the lone wolf, and the next round begins.

### *Strategies*

For Tommy (Mr. Wolf):

- Do not focus on catching many people every time he calls, "Lunch time!" Instead, focus on just two or three (or sometimes even one).
- Aim for runners that he has a good chance of catching; if he wants a challenge, aim for faster runners.
- Pretend to chase Jada, then go after another runner.
- Keep calling time numbers until the runners are close enough to him that he has a reasonable chance of tagging them.
- Remain ambiguous and avoid any clues that he is about to call, "Lunch time!"

For Jada (runner):

- Start behind the line in an area relatively far from Tommy but still within the game's designated boundaries; thus Tommy will have to run a longer distance to tag her.
- Maintain the ready position and always be prepared to sprint back to the start line.

# TAG VARIATIONS

Numerous tag-like games and variations can be found; the ones described here make up just a small sampling of the many possibilities this game provides. Rachel, a 7-year-old girl, describes a variation that she and her friends play: "We're sort of making up games that we have to play tag backwards so we have to walk backwards. . . . So it's going to be a little harder. Like somebody's walking backwards and they see somebody in front of them, and so they walk backwards to tag the person, but the other person can't see them. So it's sort of a little tricky tag." In addition, many fantasy games (superheroes or other role-playing games) (Jarrett, Farokhi, Young, & Davies, 2001) employ tag rules and strategies.

Some variations of tag are physically demanding; that is, they require excellent running and dodging skills that may make it difficult for children with less movement competence to remain involved. As Josh (an 8-year-old with a physical disability) says, "Yeah, I don't like games, games of tag, be . . . beca . . . because I'm always, like, It." Tristan (age 8) explains the problem this way:

> [Being a poor runner] is not fun for the person who's It. It's [also] not fun for the people who are not It because people who are not It sometimes want to be It, chasing people. . . . But . . . if one person's It all the time and nobody else gets to be It and one person's chasing a whole bunch of people for the whole game, it's not very fun. Like, would you like being It chasing four people and being It the whole time? . . . That's not fun for anybody, 'cause if people are being chased by the same person, they're going to get tired of running and . . . tired of running away from the same person.

Some variations of tag (such as that described by Rachel), reduce the need for running skill and replace it with a novel skill (e.g., walking backward) or add another skill (e.g., throwing a ball at someone) which may level the playing field for the less competent runner. As 7-year-old Kate describes, special strategies may also help reduce the advantage of the very skillful children in the group by making the job of identification harder.

> We're playing this game—like it's people count to 50, but it's not hide-and-go-seek—count to 50 and you have to touch—do it around the pole and the other kids go hide and we sort of trick them because we put each other's coats on, and they have to touch the pole and say 1-2-3 on Kate or Lorena or something.

Identifying Kate, when she is wearing Lorena's coat, challenges other skills than the physical!

# GAMES USING TAG CONCEPTS

Elements of tag such as visual scanning, balance, ready position, and strategy transfer to many more complicated games played by older children, adolescents, and even adults. If children increase their ability to play tag through practice and participation in its variations, they will stand a better chance of being able to play other games as they get older. Games such as softball and touch football involve quick changes in direction or speed, faking, and moving skillfully and efficiently into and out of the ready position. These strategies are, of course, practiced in the game of tag and its variations (Belka, 1998). In touch football, the ball carrier's strategies are very much like those of the Not-It person (i.e., Jada) in tag—avoid getting caught while advancing. Similarly, the defender in touch football has the same responsibility faced by the person serving as It (i.e., Tommy) in tag when he or she tries to approach the ball carrier by restricting the space for movement, cutting off forward progress, and even cornering the ball carrier between the defender and the sideline.

Equipment tag shares strategic elements with other standard sports. The thrower attempts to tag an opponent by throwing a ball at him or her, and the dodger attempts to avoid being hit. Similarly, hockey, soccer, and American football all exhibit aspects of British bulldog, in that players attempt to advance from one location to another without being successfully approached (i.e., tackled, interfered with, or impeded) by opponents. And capture the flag is similar to hide-and-seek tag, as players try to hide from opponents and return to a safe base.

# TEACHING TAG SKILLS

You can help your child learn basic tag strategies that apply to many tag variations—and to a number of more advanced games that children play as they grow up. In its many variations, tag is almost certainly the most common simple game played on the playground; as such, it is well worth teaching. You can alter the game complexity as children grow and their interests expand, thus preparing them for other activities in which they may eventually participate (Amberg, 1993). In all four types of tag, players should

- leave themselves two or more escape routes so they do not get trapped;
- use deceptive techniques such as (for runners) hiding and quickly changing directions and (for chasers) looking at or feinting toward one runner but pursuing or throwing at another;
- put someone or something between themselves and the chaser to reduce the chance of being tagged;
- run (or throw) to where the runners will be, not to where they currently are, when chasing; and
- (in capture the flag) wait for the chaser to pursue someone else before making a run for it (similarly, in football and soccer, children should be as far away from opponents as possible while still remaining in a good open position).

Preschool children and those with developmental disabilities, in particular, may benefit from learning the rules and strategies of tag in stages. Take on one rule or strategy at a time and use it in an activity that will prepare the children for the next level of the game. For these children, the following sequence of instructional games may help.

- **Chase.** The object of this activity is to learn to escape. Initially, the teacher or instructor chases the children; when tagged, each child sits down until all have been caught. Alternately, two or three children can chase the others until all have been caught.
- **Catch one, catch all.** The object of this activity is for everyone who is tagged to become an It until the whole group consists of Its and there is no one left to chase. This game helps children gradually grasp the concept and meet the challenges of dealing with multiple Its.
- **Tiny tag.** The object here is to play the fundamental game of tag in small groups so that each child changes roles frequently. One child is It and chases only a few others in a small or limited space until they are caught. The teacher or leader can systematically increase the number of people being chased as the children learn the game. At this stage, the children learn that they do not want to be It and should avoid being tagged.
- **Basic tag.** Since the role of It rotates continuously in this game, children must learn that when they are tagged they become It and when they tag someone they are no longer It. Teachers and parents can restrict the designated game space to give a slow runner who is It a better chance of tagging someone within a reasonable amount of time. To avoid having the same person become It repeatedly, the leader can designate a safe area (e.g., a big tire swing), a safe position (e.g., crouching), or a safe movement (e.g., jumping jacks) that makes a runner immune to being tagged. Rules can also dictate that several other children must serve as It before a previously tagged person can be tagged again.
- **Freeze tag.** This game involves more rules. When children are caught, they must stand frozen (or in some defined position) until someone who is not It touches them. At first, the adult leader can release those who are frozen; eventually, the children can release each other.

# CONCLUSION

Many different games are played on the playground every day. For children, these playground games can be serious business. They are important. After all, what adult cannot vividly remember at least some of his or her joyful—or, perhaps, painful—experiences in playground games? These games give children opportunities for the important social interactions that help them make friends, feel included, and gain credibility and status as part of the playground community.

Tag is a very common playground game among both girls and boys, and it comes in many variations played throughout the school years. To make sure that children can be included in this common activity, parents, leaders, and instructors should spend time understanding its demands and teaching its skills and strategies. Such guidance enhances the playground experience for children who play tag every day; in addition, participating in games of tag may also help children develop a strong foundation for better performance in more complex games played by older children.

# Bibliography

Amberg, J.M. (1993). Tag: Make it new and useful. *Strategies, 7*(2), 14–16.

Ames, C. (1992). Achievement goals, motivational climate, and motivational processes. In G.C. Roberts (Ed.), *Motivation in sport and exercise* (pp. 161–176). Champaign, IL: Human Kinetics.

Bandura, A. (1986). *Social foundations of thought and action: A social cognitive theory.* Englewood Cliffs, NJ: Prentice Hall.

Belka, D.E. (1998). Strategies for teaching tag games. *Journal of Physical Education, Recreation and Dance, 69*(8), 40–45.

Blatchford, P., Baines, E., & Pellegrini, A. (2003). The social context of school playground games: Sex and ethnic differences, and changes over time after entry to junior school. *British Journal of Developmental Psychology, 21*, 481–505.

Bouffard, M. (2003). Foundations of assessment. In R.D. Steadward, G.D. Wheeler, & E.J. Watkinson (Eds.), *Adapted physical activity* (pp. 163–173). Edmonton: University of Alberta Press.

Bouffard, M. (1993). The perils of averaging data in adapted physical activity research. *Adapted Physical Activity Quarterly, 10*(3), 371–391.

Bouffard, M., & Dunn, J. (1993). Children's self-regulated learning of movement sequences. *Research Quarterly for Exercise and Sport, 64*, 393–403.

Bouffard, M., Watkinson, E., Thompson, L., Causgrove Dunn, J., & Romanow, S. (1996). A test of the activity deficit hypothesis with children with movement difficulties. *Adapted Physical Activity Quarterly, 13*(1), 61–73.

Bruner, J.S. (1983). *Child's talk: Learning to use language.* New York: Norton.

Burton, A.W., & Davis, W.E. (1996). Ecological task analysis: Utilizing intrinsic measures in research and practice. *Human Movement Science, 15*, 285–314.

Burton, A., & Miller, D. (1998). *Movement skill assessment.* Champaign, IL: Human Kinetics.

Causgrove Dunn, J. (2003). Considering motivation. In R.S. Steadward, G.D. Wheeler, & E.J. Watkinson (Eds.), *Adapted physical activity* (pp. 325–344). Edmonton: University of Alberta Press.

Causgrove Dunn, J., & Watkinson, E.J. (2001). Perceptions of self and environment as mediators of participation in physical activity: Considering motivation theory in the study of Developmental Coordination Disorder. In S.A. Cermak & D. Larkin (Eds.), *Developmental Coordination Disorder* (pp. 185-199). Albany, NY: Delmar.

Causgrove, J.L., & Watkinson, E.J. (1994). A study of the relationship between physical awkwardness and children's perceptions of physical competence. *Adapted Physical Activity Quarterly, 11*(3) 275–283.

Corbin, C.B., & Pangrazi, R.P. (1998). *Physical activity for children: A statement of guidelines.* Reston, VA: National Association for Sport and Physical Education.

Davis, W.E., & Broadhead, G.D. (2007). *Ecological task analysis and movement.* Champaign, IL: Human Kinetics.

Davis, W.E., & Burton, A.W. (1991). Ecological task analysis: Translating movement behavior theory into practice. *Adapted Physical Activity Quarterly, 8*(2), 154–177.

Davis, W., & van Emmerik, R. (1995). An ecological task analysis approach for understanding motor development in mental retardation: Philosophical and theoretical underpinnings. In A. Vermeer, & W. Davis (Eds.), *Physical and Motor Development in Mental Retardation* (Medicine and Sport Science Series ed., Vol. 40, pp. 1–32). Karger: Basel.

Duda, J. (1987). Toward a developmental theory of children's motivation in sport. *Journal of Sport Psychology, 9,* 130–145.

Eccles, J., Wigfield, A., & Schiefele, U. (1998). Motivation to succeed. In W. Damon & N. Eisenberg (Eds.), *Handbook of child psychology* (5th ed., Vol. 3, pp. 1017–1095). New York: Wiley.

Evans, J., & Roberts, G. (1987). Physical competence and the development of children's peer relations. *Quest, 39*(1), 23–35.

Fitzpatrick, D.A., & Watkinson, E.J. (2003). The lived experience of physical awkwardness: Adults' retrospective views. *Adapted Physical Activity Quarterly, 20*(3), 279–297.

Harter, S. (1981). The development of competence motivation in the mastery of cognitive and physical skills: Is there a place for joy? In G.C. Roberts & D.M. Landers (Eds.), *Psychology of motor behaviour and sport, 1980* (pp. 3–29). Champaign, IL: Human Kinetics.

Jarrett, O.S., Farokhi, B., Young, C., & Davies, G. (2001). Boys and girls at play: Recess at a southern urban elementary school. In S. Reifel (Ed.), *Theory in context and out.* Westport, CT: Ablex.

Lee, D.T., & Magill, A.R. (1983). The locus of contextual interference in motor-skill acquisition. *Journal of Experimental Psychology, 9*(4), 730–746.

Lever, J. (1978). Sex differences in the complexity of children's play and games. *American Sociological Review, 43,* 471–483.

Lloyd, M., Reid, G., & Bouffard, M. (2006). Self-regulation of sport specific and educational problem-solving tasks by boys with and without DCD. *Adapted Physical Activity Quarterly, 23,* 370–389.

Magill, R. (1998). *Motor learning: Concepts and applications.* New York: McGraw-Hill.

National Association for Sport and Physical Education. (2007). Active Start: A statement of physical activity guidelines for children birth to five years. www.aahperd.org/naspe/template.cfm?template = ns_active.html.

National Association of Early Childhood Specialists in State Departments of Education. (2001). Recess and the importance of play: A position statement on young children and recess. (ERIC Document Reproduction Service No. ED463047).

Nichols, J.G. (1989). *The competitive ethos and democratic education.* Cambridge, MA: Harvard University Press.

Pellegrini, A. (2005). *Recess: Its role in education and development.* Hillsdale, NJ: Erlbaum.

Schmidt, R.A., & Wrisberg, C.A. (2004). *Motor learning and performance: A problem-based learning approach* (3rd ed.). Champaign, IL: Human Kinetics.

Spencer-Cavaliere, N., Causgrove Dunn, J. & Watkinson, E.J. (2009). Is recess an achievement context? An application of expectancy-value theory to playground choices. *The Alberta Journal of Educational Research, 55*(1).

Sweeting, T., & Rink, J.E. (1999). Effects of direct instruction and environmentally designed instruction on the process and product characteristics of a fundamental skill. *Journal of Teaching in Physical Education, 18,* 216–233.

Thompson, L., Bouffard, M., Watkinson, E., & Causgrove Dunn, J. (1994). Teaching children with movement difficulties: Highlighting the need for individualized instruction in regular physical education. *Physical Education Review, 17*(2), 152–159.

Wall, A.E. (2004). The developmental skill-learning gap hypothesis: Implications for children with movement difficulties. *Adapted Physical Activity Quarterly, 21*, 197–218.

Watkinson, E.J., & Causgrove Dunn, J. (2003). Applying ecological task analysis to the assessment of playground skills. In Steadward, R., Wheeler, G., & Watkinson, E.J. *Adapted Physical Activity* (pp. 229–253). Edmonton, Alberta: University of Alberta Press.

Watkinson, E.J., & Muloin, S. (1988). Playground skills of moderately mentally handicapped youngsters in integrated elementary schools. *The Mental Retardation and Learning Disability Bulletin, 16*(2), 3–13.

Watkinson, E.J., & Wall, A.E. (1982a). *The PREP play program: Play skill instruction for mentally handicapped children*. Ottawa: Canadian Association for Health, Physical Education and Recreation.

Watkinson, E.J., & Wall, A.E. (1982b). *The PREP program: A preschool play program for moderately mentally retarded children*. Ottawa: Canadian Association for Health, Physical Education and Recreation.

Watkinson, E.J., Causgrove Dunn, J., Cavaliere, N., Calzonetti, K., Wilhelm, L., & Dwyer, S. (2001). Engagement in playground activities as a criterion for diagnosing developmental coordination disorder. *Adapted Physical Activity Quarterly, 18(1)*,18–34.

Watkinson, E.J., Dwyer, S.A., & Nielsen, A.B. (2005). Children theorize about reasons for recess engagement: Does expectancy-value theory apply? *Adapted Physical Activity Quarterly, 22*(2), 179–197.

Wigfield, A., & Eccles, J. (2002). The development of competence beliefs, expectancies for success, and achievement values from childhood through adolescence. In A. Wigfield & J. Eccles (Eds.), *Development of achievement motivation* (pp. 91–120). San Diego: Academic Press.

# Index

*Note:* The italicized *f* and *t* following page numbers refer to figures and tables, respectively.

# About the Author

**Jane Watkinson, PhD**, is the dean of faculty of kinesiology and recreation management at the University of Manitoba in Winnipeg, Manitoba. Before her role as dean, she was the associate dean academic from the faculty of physical education and recreation at the University of Alberta in Edmonton, Alberta. Dr. Watkinson earned the McCalla Award from the University of Alberta and CAHPER Scholar Award during her career. In her free time, she enjoys playing squash, racquetball, and the piano.

# About the Illustrator

**Terry Watkinson** earned the challenging BSc degree in medical illustration and went on to teach surgical illustration and perspective for the University of Toronto's biomedical communications program. His illustrations are featured in many medical textbooks and journals. Terry is now an artist and illustrator living in Winnipeg, Manitoba, Canada, where he creates a brilliant sense of light, depth, and emotion in his spectacular wilderness scenes and cityscapes.

You'll find other outstanding
recreation resources at
# www.HumanKinetics.com

# How to Use the CD-ROM

## SYSTEM REQUIREMENTS

You can use this CD-ROM on either a Windows-based PC or a Macintosh computer.

### *Windows*

- IBM PC compatible with Pentium processor
- Windows 98/2000/XP/Vista
- Adobe Reader 8.0
- Microsoft Word
- 4x CD-ROM drive

### *Macintosh*

- Power Mac recommended
- System 10.4 or higher
- Adobe Reader
- Microsoft Word for Mac
- 4x CD-ROM drive

## USER INSTRUCTIONS

### *Windows*

1. Insert the *Let's Play!* CD-ROM. (Note: The CD-ROM must be present in the drive at all times.)
2. Select the "My Computer" icon from the desktop.
3. Select the CD-ROM drive.
4. Open the file you wish to view. See the "00Start.pdf" file for a list of the contents.

### *Macintosh*

1. Insert the *Let's Play!* CD-ROM. (Note: The CD-ROM must be present in the drive at all times.)
2. Double-click the CD icon located on the desktop.
3. Open the file you wish to view. See the "00Start" file for a list of the contents.

For customer support, contact Technical Support:

Phone: 217-351-5076 Monday through Friday (excluding holidays) between 7:00 a.m. and 7:00 p.m. (CST).
Fax: 217-351-2674
E-mail: support@hkusa.com